Manage
Your Financial Life

Manage
Your Financial Life

JUST STARTING OUT

NANCY DOYLE

ISBN 978-0-9976097-2-1

Note: The information I provide in this book is provided only as a source of information. This book and the information provided in it is not intended to be used as the basis for investment decisions, and nothing in this book should be considered a solicitation to buy any particular financial instrument or security. You have to make your own investment decisions based on your specific financial needs, goals, and risk tolerance.

Contents

Preface

ONGRATULATIONS! You are more or less "launched" and on your own. Independence, self-reliance, and freedom are your new reality. And, as you well know, this new reality also entails meeting deadlines, doing chores, and taking care of your home.

Finances also play a big role in your new reality. Older generations have probably reiterated the importance of establishing prudent financial habits when you are young. You may have already realized that your "finances" are more intricate than simply collecting a paycheck and paying your bills and that managing your financial life is about more than just monitoring expenses and using debt wisely. Managing your financial life is not just about sticking to a budget or making a savings plan. Managing your financial life is also about being organized, being informed, taking a comprehensive view of your finances, and figuring out what to do with your money—and how to invest it. Just like you need to take care of your career, your health, your emotional well-being, and your relationships, you need to take care of your financial life.

I have been in the finance and investing world for more than thirty years. I know firsthand that people of all ages and stages of life want to learn about finance and investing. Often they don't know how or where to start. Over the years, friends and family have reached out to me with questions about personal finance. In many instances, these people were going through a life transition with a financial impact—buying a home, getting married, having children, changing careers, starting a business, getting divorced, losing a spouse. Such transitions often serve as catalysts to motivate people to become more engaged in their finances. Frequently, I am asked to recommend resources to help someone become more knowledgeable. I have never found a resource offering comprehensive, easy-to-understand, objective, and helpful ways to learn how to manage one's financial life.

Although I am a "numbers" person, my jobs have always entailed a lot of writing, which I enjoy. The idea to write my first book, which is about personal finance for women, was hatched five years ago over lunch with a college roommate. She asked me to explain the meaning behind some financial jargon, and then she suggested that because I had a knack for explaining things in an easy-to-understand manner, I should consider writing a book. She has spent her career in book publishing, so her suggestion stuck with me. After thinking about it for a while, I agreed to write the book under one condition: that she work with me. She is a brilliant editor, but she is not naturally a financial person, and I think we make a great team.

When *Manage Your Financial Life: A Thoughtful, Organized Approach for Women,* came out in November 2016, the feedback was wonderful. I was surprised by how many men also read it and enjoyed it. From both women and men, the most common comment I received was a request: "Will you please write a book for my son or daughter who is just starting out in the workforce?" That was the inspiration for this, my second book.

For my generation and older, we think of "just starting out" as one's early years in the workforce and the milestones encountered—first couple of jobs, first couple of homes, grad school, getting engaged, starting a family, and so on. Your milestones and your financial circumstances will be unique. For that reason, the topics I cover are broad. You may have just graduated from college, or you may be in your mid-thirties and just starting to think about long-term financial goals. You may have a broad knowledge of financial concepts, or you might not know much more than what a checking account and a credit card are. Some of the topics in this book may apply to you and your situation, and some may not.

Many of the "real life experiences" that I shared in the first book came from my life as a young adult. When I was "just starting out," my financial life was different than my parents' had been when they had started out in the workforce—just as the financial world you face today is different than the one I faced many years ago.

Although the financial world looks very different than it did when I graduated from college, my approach to managing one's financial life works no matter what the era. It worked for my parents' generation, it works for my generation, and it will work for your generation. The concepts and exercises laid out in this book withstand the test of time. You can use them to implement a plan—which I also suggest—to take control of your financial life.

The first step in the plan is to get organized. For most of us, time is a precious commodity. Organization is essential for managing day-to-day tasks, being disciplined, and achieving goals. Part of being organized in your financial life is implementing a system for tracking your financial information. Keeping records, whether they are paper or electronic, is more complicated in today's world than it was in the past. Whether they are account statements, tax information, proxies and other regulatory notices, or marketing materials, information in both paper and electronic formats bombards us on a daily basis. Most people hang onto things—in both paper and electronic formats—that don't really matter much. As a result, they often cannot find what they need when they need it. Having a system for organizing your important files and documents will help you pare down your "stuff" and manage your finances more efficiently.

After getting organized, the next steps in the plan are to analyze your financial profile objectively, to learn about investing, and then to put it all together and invest your money. To analyze your situation and implement a plan effectively, you must take a comprehensive view of your situation. My hope is that this book will help you take an honest, objective view of your finances, build on your understanding of finance and investing concepts, and apply that knowledge in your everyday life.

What I propose here is a process, and it will take some time. But because you are just starting out, time is on your side. That said, establishing sound practices when you are young will have a profound impact on your financial well-being—and your ability to sleep at night.

Throughout the book, "good-to-know" sidebars and "real-life experience" sidebars complement the discussion. The good-to-know sidebars explain concepts, industry jargon, or what a saying actually means. My real-life situations will help you see how to apply the lessons in the book to your own life. I also highlight nine "golden rules." These essential, easy-to-remember rules have a profound impact on your financial well-being.

A Starting Point

The 2008 global financial crisis had a profound impact on me. Although it was stressful on many levels, my family—like many others—worked together to navigate the challenging period. What was most distressing for me was discovering how many people did not understand the various risks associated with their investments or with their personal financial profiles. The crisis had deep repercussions not only on people's finances but also on their lives. To me, it clearly illustrated the importance of being informed and thoughtful about one's finances.

The 2008 global financial crisis also sparked my interest in exploring how to help people manage their financial lives. Contrary to what you might think, you do not need to have a business degree to invest your money. My mother did not have a background in finance, but she was a successful lifelong investor. I believe there are several reasons why:

- She was encouraged to learn about investing at an early age.
- She understood the importance of saving and investing.
- She enjoyed managing her finances and stayed engaged in managing them throughout her life.

One of my main objectives in writing this book is to explain things in an approachable, easy-to-understand manner. In many instances I will "walk through the math" with you. When it comes to finance and investments, simple numerical examples go a long way to helping you understand a concept and the possible implications of your choices. Do you know the adage "the numbers don't lie"? It's true.

Even if you have a financial background, there are plenty of opportunities to continue learning. The financial world is always evolving, and your financial needs will inevitably change as you age. Your financial profile will become more complex as you advance in your career, start a family, and experience other milestones. I have a BA in economics and an MBA in finance. In my education and early career, I focused on corporate finance—how companies fund themselves. In the mid-1990s, I decided to pursue a career in the investment industry.

Until that point, most of what I had learned about investing was from my parents and my husband. My first job in the investment industry was in a research department at an investment bank, where I analyzed financial stocks.

A few years after landing my first job in the investment industry, I became a mom, and my life got a lot busier. Although I was a CFA® charterholder and licensed to buy and sell investments, I hired someone to help manage our family's money. I still use the same person I hired more than twenty years ago. Although I work with a financial adviser, I also make some investments on my own.

An Objective Perspective

When it comes to money, I believe that independence and objectivity are crucial. You will find many articles, books, and websites that cover finance and investing topics. You may discover that the author or website founder is selling financial products or is aligned with a financial firm. I am concerned that their advice may not be truly objective.

My perspective is different. I am an independent consultant, and I do not work for nor am I partnered with any financial services companies. I am not selling financial products, nor am I looking to attract new clients. I have put my education and professional experience into practice in my own life, and I am sharing my knowledge and experiences in this book. Like my parents, I regard learning about finance and investments as a lifelong pursuit, and I am always looking for ways to manage my financial life better.

In this book, I do not give financial, legal, accounting, or tax advice. Rather, I share my system for managing my financial life. Some parts of this system may work better for you than others—use only what works for you. I have certain opinions and let you know what they are. I use numbers in this book for illustrative purposes only—they do not reflect current market conditions. I encourage you to visit my website at www.manageyourfinanciallife.com and follow me on twitter@nancyfinance. Please feel free to ask questions and provide feedback. I welcome them. In addition to my articles and interviews, I am eager to share others' work that I think is informative and helpful.

There are many people who deserve thanks. Over the years, it has been an honor to work with talented people who have taught me a great deal about finance and investing. My family and friends are a wonderful source of encouragement. My book designer, Cecile Kaufman, always excels at creating just the right look. I truly appreciate my editor and great friend, Deirdre Greene, who suggested that I write my first book and agreed to take on the second one with me. My wonderful parents, who are with me in spirit, taught me and supported me in all ways. Finally, I am most grateful to Bill, Brendan, and Julia. You bring me joy and are everything to me.

Introduction

. . . .

*C*OMPARED TO YOUR parents' and grandparents' day, the financial world is vastly more complex. You have more choices, opportunities, and platforms than your parents and grandparents did, but you also shoulder a lot more responsibility. Your world is different, and so is your financial life.

In your grandparents' generation, a person often spent his or her entire career at one company. There was much more certainty than today—job security, good benefits, a comfortable retirement. Today, people change jobs frequently, often take on part-time or consulting work, and sometimes start their own businesses. According to the Bureau of Labor Statistics, millennials will have an average of seven different employers before age twenty-nine.[1] As you progress in your career, the number will continue to rise.

You conduct your financial life across multiple platforms—paper, online, mobile. Making financial transactions over the Internet and using mobile devices brings unprecedented convenience and access to real-time information regarding your accounts. Research firm eMarketer predicts that more than 90 million people will use mobile peer-to-peer (P2P) and payment apps by 2019. Forrester Research projects that the value of mobile transactions will exceed $280 billion by 2021.[2]

People just starting out often face a substantial headwind: hefty student loan payments. A study conducted by the National Association of Realtors and American Student Assistance found that student debt is causing millennials to delay financial commitments such as saving for retirement, marrying, and starting a family. According the Federal Reserve, 70 percent of college students have student loans.[3] The amount outstanding per student is up nearly 70 percent from a decade ago.[3] For people age thirty-five or younger with student loans, the average balance is $33,300.[3] In the aggregate, student debt outstanding totals $1.4 trillion,[4] which is greater than all credit card debt outstanding. This burden is challenging. More than one in ten borrowers are at least ninety days behind on their student loans—the highest delinquency rate for any form of credit.[4]

Baby boomers are the wealthiest generation in history. Over the next few decades, experts predict that they will pass down $30 trillion in assets to Gen Xers and millennials. This "great wealth transfer," as it is known, means younger generations have an added incentive to be informed about finance and investing.

In terms of saving and investment, there are many options today—a variety of investments, platforms, and types of advice and assistance. Increasingly, we are connected and interconnected. On a larger scale, as the financial world becomes ever more interconnected, global economic and market events affect all of us.

With greater choices and greater flexibility come greater uncertainty. With the plethora of options available, how do you decide what is best for you? What does all the industry jargon mean? Given the uncertainty, you need to make sure you have control over your financial life. But comfort with your financial life is not necessarily related to the size of your paycheck or what stage of life you're in.

People's financial profiles are diverse, as are their circumstances, concerns, and goals. As our lives change, so do our financial needs and outlook. The paths people take through life also vary. Every change in your life—and your financial profile—involves papers, documents, and forms. Even if you are just starting out, you likely have already accumulated files and papers—paper and electronic—that you need to retain. You may have a lease agreement, student loan documentation, retirement plan information, bank statements, credit card statements, health insurance information, or a renter's insurance policy. If you have a car, that means additional papers and documents. You also may be swamped with offers from credit card, mortgage, or insurance companies. What is important? What do you need to keep? What do you need to follow up with?

It's Time to Contemplate Your Financial Life

Regardless of your financial circumstances, now is the time to take control of your financial life. The degree of familiarity with financial concepts varies widely from person to person:

- Some people are more familiar with the variety of investments and investment accounts than others.
- Many people know something about finance and investing. Some know a lot, and some know nothing or very little.
- Some people are comfortable choosing investments for their retirement plan, some are not.

There may be many financial goals on your horizon: grad school tuition; a down payment for a home; getting married; starting a family. How do you tackle multiple savings goals at once? What about balancing goals along with your financial obligations? How do you prioritize?

Just as your goals are unique, so too may be your concerns. In addition to tackling large student loan payments, you may be wondering:

- How do I save and pay rent at the same time?
- How do I juggle or track multiple financial accounts?
- Where do I find the time to learn about investing and managing my money?
- How do I make decisions about my retirement plan?
- Will I be able to provide a life for my family like the one I had growing up?
- If I seek help or advice, can I trust it?

A Book for Those Who Are Just Starting Out

As you advance in your career and take on more responsibilities in life—buy a home, start a family, start a business—your financial profile will become more involved. Even though your financial profiles may not be complex at this point, you may feel disorganized.

My goal is to educate, engage, and empower you while helping you simplify your financial life. Some people find the subject of finances and the process of investing overwhelming; others don't know where to start or whom to trust. Getting a handle on your finances likely involves a mountain of paperwork—documents, statements, forms. Although "paperwork" is increasingly moving online, the sheer volume of financial information—whether paper or electronic—can lead to stress from feeling disorganized and overwhelmed.

The articles, books, websites, and videos on personal finance that I have encountered are often incomplete, too complicated, or overly simplistic. They might encourage people to invest, but they don't tell them how to do so effectively. The information that is out there can perpetuate the perception that investing and personal finance are overwhelming topics that are difficult to understand—and who has the time?

A Comprehensive, Coordinated Method

In terms of your financial life, there are two main questions: (1) Where are you now? and (2) Where do you want to go? To answer these questions, you must take a comprehensive view of your finances. Your financial decisions affect many areas of your life. This book presents a comprehensive, coordinated method for taking control of your financial life.

Managing your financial life encompasses the participation of your partner, if you have one. Money can be a major source of stress in relationships, and you and your partner need to be on the same page with respect to finances. Working together can help reduce stress around finances. Moreover, behavioral finance studies have shown that people tend to make better decisions about savings and investments after discussing their ideas with others, especially people with diverse viewpoints. If you have a partner, managing your finances must be a joint effort.

Some authors have written extensively about debt reduction and managing day-to-day finances but little about investing. Others have written about how to organize your life but have not focused on finance and investments. This book presents a broad discussion about managing your financial life by addressing the multiple aspects involved. Taking a comprehensive view and working through the steps are essential. There are four main steps to follow:

- Get organized.
- Analyze your financial profile.
- Educate yourself about investing.
- Save and invest your money.

You will find that it is important to do these steps in order; the steps all relate to each other.

Why is getting organized the first step? Being disorganized about your finances will have a profound impact on many areas of your life. When your financial life is disorganized, you might not understand what resources you have and where your important financial information is. You will make uninformed decisions, and you won't understand the riskiness of your financial profile. Your money might not be working for you or might even be working against you. Bad decisions resulting from being disorganized could result in missed opportunities, penalties, and extra taxes. Organizing your financial life, the topic of part 1, may take more effort than organizing other areas of your life, but the impact is profound.

Once you've organized your financial affairs, it will be time to analyze your financial profile and assess potential risks: this is the focus of part 2. Part 3 explains financial concepts and different ways to invest. This part is not intended to be a definitive explanation of these topics but understanding this information will help you be better informed and feel more confident.

Finally, it will be time to put your knowledge to work: to examine your goals, develop a savings plan, and invest your money, the subject of part 4. You must be engaged. Read, research, ask questions, and seek answers. The people who help us manage our financial lives are also paid to answer our questions. Managing your financial affairs is not something that you should ignore or postpone until you're older—now is the time to start!

Some Financial Truths

Your financial profile may seem simple when you are just starting out, but it will become more complex as you advance in your career, purchase a home, or start a family—if these are part of your plan. As you start down the path of gaining control of your financial life, here are some themes to keep in mind.

Everything Is Related

Not only must you look at your "big picture," but also keep in mind that your financial decisions are interrelated. A spending decision you make this afternoon will affect how much you can save this month. Opening a credit card this weekend will affect the rate on a car loan you take out next summer. Selling a stock today will affect the taxes you will owe next April. Pay attention to details.

Retirement Looms No Matter Your Age

For our grandparents, their employers took care of investing their pension, and the government was responsible for their Social Security benefits. In today's model, the vast majority of individuals do not have traditional pensions. The primary source of retirement income comes from 401(k) plans, 403(b) plans, and individual retirement accounts. Traditional sources of retirement funds need to be supplemented by personal investments. Because you, not your employer or the government, are ultimately responsible for your retirement, managing your money for today and tomorrow is a task that you cannot take lightly.

It may be tempting to borrow from your retirement plans to help pay for grad school or for a down payment on a home. Even though you are young, you must make retirement a priority. If you don't prioritize saving and investing for retirement now, you risk not having enough money to retire when the time comes, and, if you have children down the road, you may end up depending on them for financial support later in life.

Managing Your Finances Should Be a Lifelong Pursuit

Saving and investing should be lifelong pursuits, and you are never too young to start. My parents taught me and my siblings about the importance of saving and investing—essential habits that are best established early. Saving for retirement through your employer as soon as possible and taking advantage of corporate matches are imperative. It is easier to put money away when you are single than when you have a family to take care of. My parents also taught us to think about giving back or investing in others.

Some of the most successful, well-respected investors in the world are in their seventies, eighties, or older. Many have accumulated significant wealth yet keep working because they enjoy what they are doing. Investing keeps them engaged. Lifelong investors don't stop reading the *Wall Street Journal* just because they have turned eighty.

A Few More Points

In this book, I address a broad range of topics and concepts. As you work through the process and become more conversant with financial concepts, many financial truths are worth remembering:

- The importance of time: Compounding is powerful.
- The importance of risk and return: There are many types of risk.
- The importance of discipline and conviction: Stay true to your plan.
- The importance of patience: Study your investment decisions and don't rush.
- The importance of value: Value is not what you paid for something. It is what someone else is willing to pay for it.

- The importance of supply and demand: Both have an impact on value.
- The importance of expectations: They also drive value.
- The importance of liquidity: How easily something can be converted to cash is key.
- The importance of total return: Look at both appreciation and income.
- The importance of taxes: Timing and keeping good records are essential.
- The importance of fees: They can really add up, especially over time.
- The importance of inflation: It affects your future spending.

The importance of people: The person managing your money, the person managing the fund that you have invested in, and the person managing the company that you invested in all matter.

When it comes to your finances, you must be honest with yourself or you will not be successful and achieve your goals. Try to look at your financial picture the same way an objective outsider would. How risky is your profile? What are your opportunities to grow assets? Are you on track to meet your goals? Learn from your mistakes. Look at what did not turn out well for you, figure out why, learn from it, and move on.

Being disciplined and informed regarding your financial affairs will allow you to "live a little." Don't forget the occasional splurge. Focus on one or two things that bring you joy. As you plan for an occasional splurge, prioritize. Saving for retirement should be a primary long-term goal, but don't forget to plan for things that bring you happiness in the short run.

It's time to get started!

PART 1

Get Organized

Organizing is what you do before you do something, so
that when you do it, it is not all mixed up.

—A. A. MILNE

Even if your financial profile is fairly simple, being organized

is essential. Your financial life involves a lot of information

and documents—both paper and electronic. Being organized

not only reduces stress, but it also helps you be more

successful managing your finances. This section addresses

how to organize your financial life, giving you tips on

determining what information you need to keep and how

you should keep it.

CHAPTER 1

· ·

Spring–Cleaning

To MANAGE YOUR financial life, you must take a comprehensive view. The first step in getting organized is to do what
I call a financial spring-cleaning. When you go through your
closet and drawers and toss or donate clothes you don't need,
you create a sense of order for your wardrobe. You can do the
same with your financial life.

A financial spring-cleaning may seem like a big task, but it does
not have to be if you have a plan. Start by gathering all papers and
documents related to your financial life. Instead of T-shirts, sweat-
ers, or jeans, gather everything related to your bank accounts,
investments, insurance policies, loans, home or apartment, and
car. This is an easy task to put off, so consider making an appoint-
ment with yourself and committing to this project. Look at the
weather forecast and pick a rainy day to get started.

Spring-cleaning may seem daunting at first, but you will begin
to see benefits right away. Everyone that I have encouraged to
undertake a financial spring-cleaning has thanked me for the
push. After you've gone through your financial documents and
put them in order, you will be more engaged in your financial

life, you will waste less time looking for things, your computer will be less cluttered, and you can avoid lugging around nonessential papers and documents when you move.

Step 1: Get Ready

We all have both paper and electronic information to organize. The steps are essentially the same for both. I use the words "document" and "folder" to mean either paper or electronic formats. For paper files, designate an area of a room where you can gather and sort the materials. For online files, keep a log of what you've dealt with as you make progress.

Put out bins for recycling and a bag for documents that you decide to shred. You will also want a stapler, a staple remover, sticky notes, pencils, paper clips, and file folders on hand.

Step 2: Gather Documents

Every change in your life—graduation, first job, new apartment, second job—involves paperwork and documents. Financial regulations require firms to send far more information and disclosures to account holders than in the past. Even if you are young and in your first job after school, it is likely that you have many more documents and statements than you realize.

· ·

I am often asked why we need to save any paper at all as we increasingly move to a paperless world. Although paperless statements save time and effort—no statements to open, file, and eventually shred— and are a much better option for the environment than paper statements, there are reasons to keep some documents in paper form. Financial firms often archive electronic documents for only a certain number of years—but you might need information beyond that window at some point. Check with your financial firms and confirm how far back they retain electronic records. Also, what if you save your documents only on your hard drive and something happens to your laptop? Be diligent about backing up your files. To be safe, keep your year-end statements and summaries in paper form.

. . . .

Gather all your documents relating to financial, tax, and legal matters, including:

- Bank, financial, and credit card accounts
- Insurance policies
- Leases
- Mortgage, car loans, student loans, or other debts
- Tax returns and supporting information
- Wills, powers of attorney, health care directives
- Information related to your home and major purchases

I assure you that your financial spring-cleaning will bring surprises. First and foremost, you will discover how much you *don't* need to keep. Second, you will uncover things that you thought were lost, and maybe even some surprises—unused gift cards, anyone?

Even doing a financial spring-cleaning of your computer makes you feel lighter and less stressed. It is easy to accumulate files on your hard drive, and you need to clean out and organize these documents from time to time. Just like for your paper files, getting rid of things that you don't need to retain on your hard drive makes it much easier to locate what you do need.

As I say: "Out of the mailbox does not mean out of mind." Check your online banking, credit card, investment, and retirement account statements on a regular basis. It is your money— keep an eye on it. Don't check your investment and retirement accounts too often, however. The markets can move day to day, and you should be focused on the long run, not on short-term fluctuations in account balances.

Step 3: Sort through Things

People who are disciplined about shopping often apply the "one in, one out" rule. For every new piece of clothing or pair of shoes they buy, they donate or discard one item. People who adopt this rule have an easier time getting ready for work and going out with friends, because their wardrobe truly works for them. The same is true for your finances.

An essential part of the financial spring-cleaning is figuring out what you should keep and what you should not. Here are some general guidelines that I follow:

What to Keep

- Keep tax returns and all supporting documents for seven years from the date that you file your taxes, not seven years from December 31st for a particular tax year.
- Keep all bank statements and credit card annual statements and summaries for the same seven-year window.
- Keep receipts for any major purchases and for all things that are insured as long as you have the item.
- Keep student loan, car loan, and mortgage documents (including payoff notices) and documentation for any other loans indefinitely.
- If you own your home or condo, keep records related to the purchase or sale and any improvements that affect the home's value indefinitely.

- Keep a record of the purchase or the confirmation for every new investment. Keep information regarding the cost basis and the date of purchase for as long as you hold the investment.
- Keep year-end statements for each investment account as long as you own investments in that account.

Keeping an orderly and logical filing system will make your life much easier when you sell an asset, such as an investment or your condo. When you make an investment or buy real estate, you need to keep a record of the date of purchase and the price you paid, otherwise known as the original cost basis. For your house or condo, any improvements that enhance its value also increase the cost basis. Keeping good records of improvements also saves time when you decide to put your home on the market and document enhancements for prospective buyers. If you invest in a mutual fund and reinvest any distributions such as dividends or capital gains, that will change the cost basis. Keeping track of the cost basis of any asset—such as an investment or your home—is essential because it determines whether or not you have a gain. A **gain** is the difference between what you sell something for and what you paid for it. The smaller the gain, the lower the taxes owed.

If you move investments to a new account at a different firm, you will need the cost basis information and dates of purchase. You need to keep statements from the old firm as long as you own the investments that have been transferred to the new firm.

What to Get Rid Of

Perhaps even more important than what you keep is what you can shred, recycle, or delete. Keeping unnecessary information and statements makes it harder to locate important information in a hurry. Most of us waste a lot of time trying to find things on our computer and amidst our papers. Getting rid of unnecessary

Opt Out of Prescreened Offers

Although our financial lives are increasingly moving online, financial firms continue to send mail. These marketing materials often include personal information. Preapproved credit card solicitations and convenience checks from your credit card company could lead to identity theft. You can opt out of prescreened offers by visiting www.optoutprescreen.com. On the site, there are fields where you can input your Social Security number and birthdate. Since neither are necessary to opt out, don't provide that information. You can also request that your credit card company not send you convenience checks.

documents frees up precious space in your file drawer and on your hard drive. Keep both a recycle bin and a shredding bin near your desk or wherever you pay bills or go through mail.

Shred or delete monthly statements once you receive year-end summaries for your investment accounts.

Shred anything with identifying information that you no longer need. Bill stubs, credit card solicitations, even prescription drug labels and instructions contain identifying information. If you are ever in doubt, shred.

During your financial spring-cleaning, you will have a lot of paper and documents to recycle or shred. If you have a significant amount to shred, consider using a professional shredding service. A professional shredder is secure—you can watch them put your materials in a massive shredding machine. It is also good for the environment, because everything gets recycled. Professional shredding saves a lot of time and is not expensive. Some communities even have document destruction events that are free.

Step 4: Implement a System for Keeping Track of Your Information

If you are busy or in a rush, you may not take the time to put important papers or computer files in a logical place. Having a system—one that makes sense for you—is essential. If you don't have a system that is easy for you to maintain, your financial spring-cleaning will be a waste of time. Your system should include both paper file folders and electronic files. I recommend that you organize paper and online files in a consistent manner. As you get older and your financial life becomes more complex, you will be glad that your system is logical, orderly, and consistent.

For the personal and financial documents that you are keeping—paper and electronic—make a separate folder for each of the following:

- Current year taxes (prior year taxes can be stored elsewhere)
- Bank accounts
- Investments (one folder for each investment or account)
- Health insurance (for the policy and to track claims)
- Other insurance policies (a separate folder for homeowners or renters, auto, life, and disability)
- Home and maintenance (for provider contacts and for receipts or invoices from renovations or significant repairs)
- Cars
- Receipts for any big-ticket purchases like electronics or appliances

With your paper and your electronic documents, make sure that your information is secure. Password-protect computer files, especially those relating to your financial affairs. Store vital papers, such as birth certificates, wills, Social Security cards, and passports, in a fire-safe box at home or a safety deposit box at your bank. Storing vital papers is covered in the next chapter.

Other Topics for Your Financial Spring-Cleaning

Passwords. Just as we are inundated with financial documents and marketing materials, the number of passwords we have—and need to keep track of—has exploded. Your passwords need to be secure. If you write them on a piece of paper, keep it out of sight and away from your computer. Think about using a pass phrase that will be easy for you to remember. The longer a password or pass phrase, the harder it is to crack.

Consider using a password management service, which stores your passwords securely online. You enter all your passwords into the service's website. When you are logging in to a site, you just enter a master password rather than entering your log-in and password for each website you visit. The sites will flag any of your passwords that are not secure and suggest you revise them. If you have a partner, a password management service can help you work together more successfully. If one partner changes a password in a hurry, it will be saved automatically.

The security of your passwords is a top priority. If you want to work with a password manager service, do your homework. Look at user reviews in the tech magazines. You could also ask someone in your IT department at work for a recommendation.

Although it may seem like a big timesaver, never instruct your browser to save a password. It is not secure. If your laptop is stolen, someone could access your accounts.

Taxes. Preparing your taxes is not a fun task. It can be significantly less unpleasant if you are organized. Your taxes involve a lot of documents, and you must keep good records. In addition to your W-2 (or 1099-Misc), you will need supporting documentation related to your investment accounts. A 1099 is a statement that details the dividends, interest, and capital gains earned during the year. Some investments are structured as partnerships and provide a year-end, or annual, K-1 instead of a 1099. A K-1 shows an investor's share of partnership income for a given year.

Financial transactions that need to be documented at tax time, occur throughout the year. Therefore, I recommend strongly that you keep a Current Year Tax folder. As you receive tax-related documents in the mail or from a financial firm's portal, store them in this paper folder or in the similar folder on your hard drive. The Current Year Tax folder is also a great place to keep track of donations and other deductible expenses that you incur during the year. The IRS's current policy for donations is that you need official documentation for all gifts greater than $250. Make a note of all donations as you make them and save all acknowledgements and thank-you emails. You may not remember a donation you made in May come tax time the next April. For more information on rules regarding donations, visit www. irs.gov/Charities-&-Non-Profits/Charitable-Organizations/ Charitable-Contributions-Written-Acknowledgments.

....

CHAPTER 2

In Case of Emergency, or ICE

*B*EING ORGANIZED IS not only about managing paper and electronic documents; it is also about having account and contact information readily available. Organizing account and contact information gives you peace of mind and will help you manage your financial life more successfully on a day-to-day basis. When life throws you a curve ball, being organized takes on even more importance. It will help you navigate challenging times more successfully.

In this section, you will prepare an "in case of emergency," or ICE, file and ICE plan. You might have emergency contact information in your phone. Some people list their main emergency contact as In Case of Emergency, or ICE. ICE preparation is not only for emergencies, but also it is key for better financial management. What if something happens to you? What if someone needs to access your email or pay bills on your behalf?

Step 1: Create an ICE File

An ICE file contains key documents that are easily accessible to you or to someone acting on your behalf. If you need to leave your house or apartment quickly—in the case of a fire, flood, or natural disaster—it is extremely helpful to have your most important documents all in one place so that you can easily access them as you leave your home.

At the least, include the following items in your ICE file:

- Legal documents, such as wills, powers of attorney, health care directives, and the titles for your home and car
- Vital records, such as birth certificates, adoption documents, marriage certificates, military records, Social Security cards, and divorce documents
- Copies of passports, credit cards, and driver's licenses

After you have gathered your vital documents, you need to put them in a safe place. Keeping these important papers in one location will save you a lot of time and makes it easier for someone who might help you in the event of an emergency. You can find fire-safe, flood-proof boxes at most hardware stores. They come in a variety of sizes and are not expensive. As an alternative, you could keep your ICE file at your bank in a safety deposit box.

. . . .

In the days before Hurricane Irma made landfall in 2017, some people posted the suggestion to keep cherished photos and key documents in the dishwasher, claiming it would be a watertight space. Fortunately, others spread the word that this was not true. An ICE file is a much better idea. Having your most important papers in one place makes it easier to find them and take them with you if you need to leave your home in a hurry.

. . . .

Step 2: Create an ICE Plan

In an ICE plan (table 2.1), you assemble key contact and financial account information in one place. An ICE plan provides guidance to someone who must act on your behalf—it is like a roadmap of your financial life. If you use a web-based personal financial management service, you have a head start on creating an ICE plan.

To create an ICE plan, prepare a list of:

- Bank accounts, credit card accounts, retirement accounts, brokerage accounts, and any other investments
- The name and phone number for anyone who helps you manage your financial life—banker, insurance agent, accountant, investment adviser
- Details about your lease or your mortgage—the name of your property management company or mortgage company
- Bills that are on automatic pay, with passwords to access the accounts or the master password if you use a password management service

TABLE 2.1. Sample ICE plan.

Company	Account Name and Notes	Account Number	Contact Info
First City Bank	Direct deposit and online bill pay	xxxxxx2209	1-800-xxx-xxxx
Credit cards	Card #1 (automatic bill pay) Card #2 (all other)	xxxx-xxxx-xxxx-4216 xxxx-xxxx-xxxx-8937	1-800-xxx-xxxx
Online Brokerage	Rollover IRA	xxxx-6147	1-800-xxx-xxxx
Asset Management Firm	Plan sponsor XYZ Corp. 401(k)	xxxx-xxxx-2345	1-800-xxx-xxxx
Jones Financial Advisers	Taxable	xxxxxx-1863	1-800-xxx-xxxx
Mutual fund	Taxable	xxxxx-7216	1-800-xxx-xxxx

(continued)

TABLE 2.1 Sample ICE plan *(continued)*.

Key contact people		
	Contact	Notes
Access to passwords	Amy Williams	Has log-in information
First City Bank Company	Tom Smith (phone number)	Downtown branch
Property management company	Meg Wilson (phone number)	Rent and maintenance issues
Insurance agent Insurance carriers	Mark James (phone number) Insurance Company #1 Insurance Company #2	City Insurance Agency Renters and auto Term life and disability
Jones Financial Advisers	Ed Jones (phone number)	
Bills on auto pay: Cable Cell		Using automatic bill pay card
Online payments for bills: Student loan payment		First City Bank's website

Some people have two credit cards: one for everyday use and one for automatic payments. If you choose to do this, after you set up automatic payments, keep the card devoted to autopay in a safe place at home. This way, if your wallet is lost or stolen, you won't have to reset all your automatic payments.

For someone just starting out, your retirement account is likely your most valuable asset. As you prepare your ICE plan, review your beneficiaries on any retirement accounts as well as on any insurance or investment accounts. This step is essential when you experience life changes—marriage, divorce, partnership, parenthood. It is good practice to review your beneficiary designations periodically, because "life happens" and things change. Your beneficiary designations must be consistent with your will. Outdated designations and inconsistencies with your will can cause big problems.

Everyone, whether single, married, or in a partnership, should designate a key person. The key person should be extremely reliable and someone whom you trust implicitly. Examples are a spouse, a partner, a parent, a sibling, or a best friend. If you have not done so already, designate your key person as a durable power of attorney. With this designation, your key person will be able to step in and manage your finances if you are not able to do so yourself. Once you designate a durable power of attorney, let the key person know about your ICE file and plan. It is also a good idea to share your email password and other main passwords with your key person. Using a password management service simplifies this process, because the key person needs only one login and master password.

Just like with your financial spring-cleaning, pulling together your ICE file and ICE plan takes some effort. As with all emergency preparation, these tools are most effective if they are in place before an emergency happens. When you are just starting out, your financial profile may seem relatively uncomplicated. Over the next few years, however, your life—and your financial life—will evolve and become more complex.

Being organized is an essential first step in managing your financial life. Get organized now. You will be glad that you did. Once you are organized, you are ready for the next step: taking an objective look at your financial profile.

PART 2

Analyze Your Financial Profile

You're in pretty good shape for the shape you are in.

— DR. SEUSS

Analyzing your finances may seem like an intimidating task. The fear of the unknown or an aversion to accountability may make you want to avoid or postpone this step. Like many things in life, though, you cannot have peace of mind or make progress toward your goals without taking an honest look at where you are now.

When you are young, you are likely juggling many commitments, financial and otherwise. This is the time to establish smart financial habits for two important reasons. First, although your plate may seem full, your financial life will likely be even more complicated in ten years, twenty years, and beyond. It is easier to ingrain sound practices now rather than later. Second, when it comes to money, time can be your friend (or your foe). Compounding investment returns over time has an enormous effect. At the same time, debts can build over the years if they are not tackled early. Financial mistakes and missed opportunities only get larger with time.

In this section, we will look at your income and your net worth. Both are key parts of analyzing your finances. We will also consider the riskiness of your financial profile and how to mitigate those risks. Everyone's financial circumstances are unique, but the concepts discussed here are useful to all.

CHAPTER 3

Analyze Your Numbers

F OR MOST PEOPLE, personal finance can be daunting. Some concepts are hard to grasp, and the future may seem a long way off. For the most part, you know what you are supposed to do. Whether you are actually doing it is a different matter. In this section, we will focus on numbers—specifically your own numbers—and take a hard look at where you are and what you need to do to get to where you want to go.

To analyze your financial profile, you need to consider your income, expenses, savings, and debts. I recommend analyzing your income and spending first. We'll then move on to your savings and your debts. After that, you can evaluate your cash flow, which connects all the components.

Watching your finances and setting spending and savings goals are as important for those just starting out as they are for people who are more established in their careers and in their lives. Sticking to a plan is another story. Just like starting a diet or joining a gym, your good intentions to stay within your spending limits may be challenged. To create a realistic plan or establish spending guidelines, you must start with an analysis of how you actually spend your money now. This analysis will help you identify habits that may hinder your success and that you may need to change.

Step 1: Create a Personal Income Statement

You must look back at the past before you can look to the future. To help figure out how you are spending the money you earn, the first step is to create a personal income statement. Then you can think about at how you should be spending money going forward.

> **Why Less Is More**
>
> When it comes to your financial accounts, more is often just more. Having too many accounts is a hassle and takes time to manage. More important, it hinders your ability to get a handle on your finances. If you have numerous bank or credit card accounts, keeping track of your day-to-day expenses—or keeping track of your debts—is challenging.

To create a personal income statement, start with your after-tax take-home pay. Add any other sources of income from consulting or part-time work (all on an after-tax basis). Next, analyze your expenses. Go to your bank's website and download your activity for the past six months. If you have a credit card, download your account activity for the same period. Look at every expense and tally up how much you spent on various categories each month. Some expenses are obvious and are the same amount month to month, such as rent, phone, and student loan payments. Other fixed recurring expenses might be utilities (cable, cell, electric, gas, water), car loan or lease payments, parking, and gym memberships.

You also incur many variable expenses every month. Although the amounts vary from month to month, these expenses occur regularly and include food, clothing, leisure activities, and other miscellaneous expenses. Other variable expenses are not as easy to estimate but can eat up your paycheck over time: daily coffee, ride-sharing services, ordering carryout, etc.

Increasingly, people are using mobile peer-to-peer, or P2P, networks to pay expenses. P2P networks allow you to pay someone directly through a mobile app without relying on cash or checks. The P2P networks make it easy for roommates to share rent, utilities, and groceries bills and are a convenient way to split tabs at restaurants and bars.

Compared to debit cards, however, P2P networks provide less detail on what you paid someone for, which can make it harder to analyze your spending. Make a habit of reviewing your P2P activity on a regular basis, such as monthly. Not only should you look at the information provided by the app, you also need to consider your P2P outlays when you download activity from your bank's website. Your bank does not provide as much information as the P2P app regarding the reason for an expense. It should be easy to identify expenses shared among roommates or larger one-time items. You should also note how much you spend on entertainment. If you don't review your activity frequently, it is harder to categorize your spending.

Use your income and expense information to create a personal income statement that shows what you earn and how you spend (table 3.1). Now look at each of your regular expenses as a percentage of your take-home pay.

Assign each expense or outlay to one of three categories:

- Essentials: things such as rent (or a mortgage), transportation, groceries, utilities, insurance, and the like
- Savings and debts: establishing an emergency fund, saving for retirement, and paying off debts
- Everything else: travel, entertainment, shopping, gifts

TABLE 3.1. Personal income statement.

Income						
Take-home pay after taxes	$45,000					

Expenses	Monthly	Annual	% of Take-home Pay	Essentials	Savings and Debts	Other
Fixed						
Rent (includes utilites)	$925	$11,100	25%	25%		
Insurance (renters, auto)	$180	$2,160	5%	5%		
Car payment	$220	$2,640	6%		6%	
Parking	$150	$1,800	4%	4%		
Cell phone	$80	$960	2%	2%		
Cable	$65	$780	2%			2%
Health club	$80	$960	2%			2%
Student loan payment	$270	$3,240	7%		7%	
		$23,640	53%			
Variable						
Food and gas	$540	$6,480	14%	14%		
Clothing, home items, etc.	$330	$3,960	9%			9%
Leisure and all other	$635	$7,620	17%			17%
		$18,060	40%			
Total expenses		$41,700	93%			
Net income		$3,300	7%		7%	
				$22,500	$9,180	$13,320
			Totals	50%	20%	30%

Totaling each category is a great diagnostic tool. It shows how you are spending your money and where you can make changes to improve your situation. Some financial planners suggest that you budget 50 percent for essential expenses, 20 percent for savings and paying down debt, and 30 percent for nonessential expenses. This practice is often referred to as the 50/20/30 rule. (Some people categorize items based on "needs" for essential outlays and "wants" for nonessential things.) Other planners simplify the rule and suggest that you aim to use 20 percent of your take-home pay for savings and paying down debt. The 20 percent rule may be easier to implement, but I prefer the 50/20/30 rule because it distinguishes between needs and wants.

MYFL Golden Rule 1
Discipline is a major factor in building net income and net worth.

When you are just starting out, your goal may be to make ends meet. It is essential to change your mindset, however. Your focus should shift to thinking about your net income and your net worth, which we will cover in the next step. Your analysis of your personal income statement and spending categories will help you make this shift. Your income (or take-home pay after tax) minus all your expenses equals your net income. To increase your net income, you must earn more than you currently do—ask for a raise, work more hours, take on a freelance gig—or you must reduce your current expenses. Focusing on net income also helps you avoid "lifestyle creep," which can happen when you increase your spending when you get a raise. If you save the extra take-home pay, your net income and net worth both increase.

There are many ways to earn or "find" extra money every month. What about housesitting or taking care of someone's pet? Tutoring? Being part of a focus group? Is there anything you could sell? Opportunities to put in extra hours at work? Maybe you could help a professional in your field manage their social media. Provide extra help around the holidays—serve at a cocktail party; set up decorations; or shop for, wrap, and ship gifts.

Looking at your recurring expenses by category helps you determine where you might be able to cut back on spending. Your rent may take up a large portion of the 50 percent allocated for essential expenses. This may be understandable in areas like New York City or the Bay Area, but it is a red flag in other locations. If the amount you spend on rent is disproportionate to where you live, plan to move to a more affordable apartment as soon as your lease is up. If you live in a high-rent market or have some time before your lease is up, you will need to reduce nonessential expenses to be able to tackle debts and save at the right level. Can you negotiate a better cell plan or drop your cable service? Can you bring your lunch to work rather than eating out every day? Learning to cook and making meals with friends rather than dining out can be a big money saver.

Your fixed and variable recurring expenses are only part of the story, however. Part of becoming financially savvy is having a plan for the unexpected. Some expenses, such as replacing a lost cell phone or minor car repairs, may be unplanned but ultimately expected. And, of course, some expenses are both unplanned and unexpected. For example, no one can predict losing power after a storm and having to replace the entire contents of their refrigerator. But not all uncertainty leads to a negative outcome. An unexpected event could result in unexpected expenses but for a positive reason. You might get engaged or need to buy a car for a great new job. Having a cash reserve is essential if you want to be prepared for unexpected situations. Establishing an emergency fund is addressed in Part 4.

You might experience an unexpected inflow, such as receiving a larger-than-anticipated tax refund or an unexpected bonus at work. Just as you should establish an emergency fund for unanticipated expenses, you should have a plan for unexpected windfalls. Be disciplined and plan for an unexpected inflow or bonus before you receive the windfall. For example, if you receive an unexpected bonus at work, you could spend 10 percent on something for yourself and save the rest. If you don't have a rule or guideline to follow, you will probably spend your windfall without having much to show for it.

Unclaimed Property—An Unexpected Inflow

Each state keeps track of unclaimed property for residents. The amount of unclaimed property—utility deposits and re-funds, unclaimed paychecks, abandoned safety deposit box-es—is surprisingly large. In some states, amounts are in the billions of dollars. Check your state treasurer's website to see if you are owed anything. You never know. . . .

Step 2: Determine Your Net Worth

The term "net worth" is frequently used to describe wealthy people, but it applies to all of us. Net worth is the total amount of your assets less the total amount of your liabilities, or debts. Creating a personal balance sheet will help you understand your net worth, and—more important—what causes your net worth to change. A balance sheet clearly illustrates how your spending and saving decisions affect your financial well-being (table 3.2). Your net worth is determined by what you earn and what you have, but it also depends on whether you spend more or less than you earn.

For managing your financial life, one of the most important formulas to remember is: Assets minus liabilities, or debts,
equals net worth. A balance sheet by definition must balance.
If your assets are greater than your liabilities, or debts, your net
worth is positive. If your liabilities, or debts, are greater than
your assets, your net worth is negative.

TABLE 3.2. Personal balance sheet.

Assets		Liabilities	
Investable assets		Secured debts	
Checking and money market	$2,000	Car loan	$12,000
Taxable investments	$17,000	Unsecured debts	
Retirement assets	$26,000	Student loans	$15,000
		Credit cards	$3,000
		Total liabilities	$30,000
Other assets			
Car	$15,000	Net worth	$30,000
Total assets	$60,000	Total liabilities and net worth	$60,000

Assets

To create your personal balance sheet, start with assets, or things
you own that are valuable. Different categories of assets are
called **asset classes.** The main types of asset classes that I focus
on here are **investable assets**, which include cash and money
market funds; US stocks; US bonds (corporate, or issued by companies; municipal, or issued by state or local governments; and
federal, or issued by the US government); international stocks;
international bonds; commodities; and currencies. Investable

assets also include funds made up of individual stocks, bonds, and the like, which are also called **securities**. (In part 3 of this book, we take a closer look at asset classes and the different types of investments and investment accounts.)

I recommend that everyone build an asset allocation grid (table 3.3). Whereas your ICE plan is a roadmap to your financial life, your asset allocation grid is like a dashboard for your financial life. All your information is in one place—easy to analyze, easy to track.

To create a grid, you can use a pencil, paper, and calculator or you can build a simple Excel spreadsheet. Look at your financial accounts—bank, investment, retirement—and note how much

TABLE 3.3. Asset allocation grid as of January X, XXXX.

	Cash/ money market	Corporate bonds	Domestic stocks	Int'l stocks	Total account	% of total assets
Checking account	$2,000				$2,000	4%
Taxable investments						
Brokerage account	$1,000		$3,000		$4,000	9%
Mutual funds	$13,000				$13,000	29%
Retirement						
401(k)		$2,000	$7,000	$3,000	$12,000	27%
IRA		$3,000	$9,000	$2,000	$14,000	31%
Total investable assets	$16,000	$5,000	$19,000	$5,000	$45,000	100%
% of total assets	36%	11%	42%	11%	100%	
By type:						
Taxable	$19,000	42%				
Retirement	$26,000	58%				
Total investable assets	$45,000	100%				

money you have in each type of asset class. The breakdown of assets by asset class is usually on the first or second page of your statements, whether they are paper or online. Using the asset allocation in each financial account, create a grid. Total the amount in each asset class at the bottom of the grid. Total the amount in each investment account on the side. Once you complete the grid, you will have your **current asset allocation.**

As you create your grid, think about the **liquidity** of your assets and your accounts. Liquidity is how easily an asset can be sold and converted to cash. Some asset classes are more liquid than others. Cash and money market funds are the most liquid assets. Stocks and bonds are fairly liquid. Retirement accounts may hold liquid investable assets, but the accounts have withdrawal restrictions and penalties and are therefore less liquid. On your asset allocation grid, put the most liquid accounts (checking and savings accounts) at the top and the least liquid accounts (retirement) at the bottom.

During a period of widespread economic turmoil—such as the 2008 financial crisis—illiquidity plays a significant role. Massive housing speculation, loose underwriting standards, and, ultimately, the inability of major financial institutions to sell, or "unwind," complex financial instruments used to fund the speculation all led to the collapse of the housing market, which in turn had an impact on both Wall Street and Main Street. For most of us, our home is our largest asset. With dramatically declining values, houses and condos were even harder to sell, or even less liquid. Many people who lost their jobs were not able to relocate for a new job because they owed more on their home than it was worth. For some, dipping into retirement savings was necessary to make ends meet, despite penalties and extra taxes. Thankfully, periods like 2008 are rare, but they do serve as a valuable lesson about the importance of monitoring your liquidity.

Okay, back to the balance sheet. The second category on your personal balance sheet is **other assets.** These include your home or condo (if you own it), car(s), and other valuable items, such as jewelry. Remember to keep appraisals and receipts for any valuable items.

Debts

Assets, regardless of the type, appear on the left side of the balance sheet. Liabilities, or debts, are listed on the right side of the balance sheet. As with assets, there are many types of debts. Debt is a complicated and often confusing topic. Not understanding how debt works can lead to costly mistakes. Visit the Consumer Financial Protection Bureau at www.consumerfinance.gov to learn more. It is important to remember that debt laws and regulations vary by state. My discussion here is a general overview of the main types of debt.

Loans you take out—or debts that you incur—are either secured or unsecured (figure 3.1). A loan is secured is if it is backed by collateral. With a secured loan, if you stop making payments on the car, home, or condo, it can be repossessed by the lender.

Unsecured debt	Secured debt
Credit card	Mortgage (first)
Bank card	Purchase money
Store card	Refinance
Student loan	Mortgage (second)
Public	Home equity loan
Private	HELOC
	Auto loan
	Car loan
	Car lease

Figure 3.1. Types of debt.

Unsecured Loans

There are two main types of unsecured loans – credit cards and student loans. Even though there is no underlying security, or collateral, to repossess, you should manage these debts very carefully. For those just starting out, unsecured debts can have a profound impact on your financial life and on your net worth.

Credit cards. The most common type of unsecured loan is credit card debt. Credit cards are a line of credit because the amount borrowed, or the amount outstanding, varies.

· ·

When I was in college, credit card companies handed out applications like candy at Halloween. Every time I bought books at the campus bookstore, there were credit card applications in the bag. Times have changed, and many full-time college students are unlikely to meet the income minimums required by credit card companies. Yet, college seniors are often offered applications. For everyone else, however, you may have to start with a credit card that carries a very low credit limit. Establish good credit history when you are young. Don't wait too long.

· ·

Misusing credit cards is one of the worst personal finance mistakes you can make. Here are some important guidelines to follow about using credit cards.

MYFL Golden Rule 2
Limit yourself to one or two credit cards.

Having more than two credit cards makes it difficult to track your spending and the amount of your total debt. People who struggle with credit card debt often have multiple cards and multiple balances outstanding. Just as it is essential to consider all your regular expenses, you need to list and track any credit card debts you have outstanding. One way to instill discipline is to allow yourself to use a credit card only for certain types of purchases, such as travel. Use your debit card (or cash) for everyday purchases and nonessential items like clothing and going out.

. . . .

My parents sent me to college with my first credit card. It was in my name, but the bills went to them. I was allowed to use it for only two things: books and emergencies. Using the credit card responsibly helped me establish good habits early in life.

. . . .

Use one or two general credit cards that provide perks that are most beneficial to you—frequent flyer miles, cash back, travel points, or other rewards. Consider the practice of using one credit card for automatic bills and keeping it in a safe place in your home. Carry a second credit card with you and use it for all other purchases.

Credit bureaus analyze your creditworthiness and assign you a credit score. Building your credit is essential when you are young, especially if you want to get a mortgage down the road. A low credit score means that you are considered a higher risk by the credit bureaus. If you have a low credit score, you will be charged a higher interest rate when you borrow money relative to lower-risk borrowers with a better credit profile. Many things can hurt your credit score, such as too much debt, opening and closing credit card accounts frequently, and late payments, or **delinquencies.** We will discuss credit scores in chapter 4.

MYFL Golden Rule 3
Never carry a credit card balance.

Credit cards are a necessary part of life. Although most adults have credit cards, most adults don't understand fully how credit cards work. You may have heard the advice "pay off your card in full each month," but do you really understand why? Using your card; generating points, miles, or whatever perks matter to you; and paying off your balance in full each month is a sound practice. You will improve your credit score by using credit responsibly. Moreover, the perks can add up. Using your card and not paying off your balance in full, however, is a very bad idea.

As with many examples in this book, let's look at the math. According to Bankrate.com, credit card interest rates, or annual percentage rates (APRs) average 16.7 percent as of this writing. If you have your first credit card, your rate will be higher—closer to 24 percent or even more. If you start the billing cycle with a balance, you are charged interest daily on the balance outstanding. If your credit card rate is 24 percent, then you are paying daily interest at a rate of $\frac{1}{365} \times 24$ percent or 0.0658 percent. If you have a $1,000 balance outstanding, you will pay $0.66 for the first day of the billing cycle. That interest is added to the balance. By the end of the first month, you will owe approximately $20 in interest, assuming that you had no other purchases on your card during the month.

Remember that for computing interest, the balance outstanding includes the amount you carry over plus any new purchases that you make during the billing cycle. In addition to the increase in your balance for daily interest charges, you will incur daily interest charges on any new purchases. If you pay off your balance every time, you begin the next billing cycle with a zero balance and will never incur interest on your purchases.

If you carry a balance, you are required to pay a minimum amount each month as indicated on your statement. Remember that the average APR for credit cards is almost 17 percent. For some credit cards, the minimum payment is as low as 1 percent of the outstanding balance plus interest accrued during the billing cycle. If you pay only the minimum amount, eliminating your credit card debt will take a very long time. Paying off more than the minimum amount should be a top priority.

Be careful with balance transfer cards. People who carry credit card debt often transfer their outstanding balance to very low or even 0 percent introductory rate cards. The attractive rate applies only to the amount transferred over to the new account. You will be charged interest on purchases made during a billing cycle; that interest is usually at a much higher rate than the rate on your balance transfer. In addition, fees are usually associated with transferring the balance. Remember that when you transfer a balance, all purchases made during a billing cycle will be charged interest.

When you make a payment on a balance transfer card, the credit card issuer will apply your minimum payment to the part of the balance with the lowest interest rate, such as a balance transferred from another card. Since the Card Act of 2009, any amount greater than the minimum payment must be applied to the part of the outstanding balance with the highest interest rate, which would include new purchases. If you cannot pay off your balance in full, this policy is a great incentive to pay off as much as possible. You will make progress chipping away at the highest-cost debt on your card—and in managing your financial life.

Student loans. Public student loans are provided by the federal government, whereas private student loans are offered by banks, credit unions, and schools. Public loans often come with lower interest rates and have more flexible terms for repayment than private loans. Student loans are unsecured—a bank cannot repossess someone's education. At the same time, student loans are usually not **discharged**, or forgiven, in a bankruptcy. That is an important distinction.

Through both traditional banks and newer, nonbank competitors, there may be opportunities to refinance student loans to achieve a lower rate. Doing so is a good idea, because the savings can be significant. Refinancing your student loan is an easy way to "find" more money each month. The difference between what you were paying and what you pay going forward can go right to savings. If you have federal loans, however, the decision whether or not to refinance is more involved. When you refinance a federal student loan, you will now have a private loan and lose the benefits associated with a federal loan. Depending on your situation, losing benefits such as income-driven repayment plans or loan forgiveness options may not be worth the lower rate.

When you refinance a student loan, make sure that you understand the terms of the new loan. The lender could offer a fixed or variable rate, and the term of the loan could be extended. Switching from a fixed to a variable rate can lower payments in the near term, but you face the risk of higher payments down the road if interest rates rise. If you extend the term of your loan, you will have lower payments because you are paying off the same amount over a longer period of time. In other words, it will take longer to pay off the loan. If you choose a variable rate option, the longer the term, the greater the chance that rates will rise and your payments will go up. There are many resources online to consult to find the best option for you. As with any loan, it is important that you understand all terms and seek recommendations for and evaluate reviews of the lender.

Secured Loans

The most common form of a secured loan is a mortgage. With a mortgage, your house or condo is the collateral. If you put 20 percent down and finance your home with a mortgage for the remaining 80 percent, the 20 percent that you put down is your **home equity.** The value of your home varies over time. Remember that the value of any asset is what someone is willing to pay for it today. Value is different than cost basis, or the purchase price you paid plus improvements. If your home declines in value to below what you owe on it, your mortgage is underwater. In other words, you have negative equity in your home.

If a borrower stops making payments on a mortgage, or **defaults**, the lender can begin foreclosure proceedings and repossess the home. When a mortgage is underwater (the balance owed exceeds the value of the home), the lender may or may not be able to recoup the difference between the value of the home and the amount owed on the loan. With a **recourse loan**, in the case of default, the lender can go after the borrower's other assets or garnish the borrower's wages. With a **nonrecourse loan**, the lender cannot go after the borrower's other assets in the case of default. It is essential to know whether your loan is recourse or nonrecourse.

Another type of secured debt is a home equity loan or line of credit. With this kind of loan, the equity in the home is the security, or collateral. As the value of your home varies over time, so does your amount of home equity. Home equity loans usually require an updated appraisal and may be a lump sum amount or may be a line of credit like a credit card. A home equity line of credit is also called a **HELOC**, and the amount borrowed varies depending on how much you use, or draw it down.

There are differences between mortgages and home equity loans. A loan that you take out to buy a home and a loan that you take out to refinance your original mortgage are both considered **first mortgages**. A home equity loan is a **second mortgage**. The first mortgage lender has priority over the second mortgage lender, or gets paid back first. If a borrower defaults and the home is repossessed, the first mortgage lender has priority and gets paid before the holder of the home equity loan does. Home equity loans are usually recourse loans, meaning the lender can go after the borrower's other assets.

Car loans and leases are secured loans. If you don't keep up with the payments, your car can be repossessed. Your car is an asset, and your car loan or lease is a debt, or liability. People may think of a car lease as an expense rather than as a debt. You should regard car leases as debts because they represent an obligation, just like a car loan or a mortgage. The monthly payment should appear as an expense on your personal income statement, and the remaining loan or lease amount should be included on your personal balance sheet as a liability, or debt.

Step 3: Focus on Cash Flow, Not Just Income

Your net income and your balance sheet both provide useful information to help you analyze your financial profile. Evaluating your cash flow takes this knowledge a step further. Unlike your net income and your personal balance sheet, cash flow takes into account changes in your savings and your debt. Changes in your debt outstanding often relate to nonessential expenses, or "wants," that are not a part of your normal budget.

In terms of your take-home pay, you either spend it, consume it, or save it. The difference between income and spending, or consumption, is your **net savings**. Your net savings depends not only on how much of your take-home pay you spend during the year but also on whether you increase or decrease the amount of debt you have outstanding in a given year.

If you . . . increase debt or dip into savings . . .	If you . . . reduce debt add to savings . . .
Then your . . . net savings and net worth decline.	Then your . . . net savings and net worth increase.

If you spend more than your take-home pay, then your debts will grow and your net worth will decline. In some years, your take-home pay and net income may be high enough to cover additional spending, but you will not be saving as much as you could otherwise. In contrast, if you decrease spending relative to income, your net worth will increase as you reduce debt or save more.

Saving for retirement, investing wisely, and managing your debts prudently should all be priorities as you take control of your financial life. Thinking about the impact of financial choices on your net worth will help you make better decisions.

MYFL Golden Rule 4

When making financial decisions, always think of the formula Assets – Liabilities, or Debts = Net Worth.

You will be more successful managing your financial life if you consider the impact of any financial decision on your net worth. Tables 3.4 and 3.5 show the impact that debt and savings

TABLE 3.4. Items affecting cash flow and net worth: decrease in net savings and net worth.		
Income	$45,000	
Net income	$3,300	
Use credit card for a few large purchases	–$5,000	
Pay down credit card with net income	$3,300	
	–$1,700	Decrease in net savings and net worth
Income	$45,000	
Less change in net savings	–$1,700	
Consumption	$46,700	Consuming more than you earn

TABLE 3.5. Items affecting cash flow and net worth: increase in net savings and net worth.

Income	$45,000	
Net income	$3,300	
Use credit card for a few large purchases	–$2,000	
Pay down debt and increase savings	$3,300	
	$1,300	Increase in net savings and net worth
Income	$45,000	
Less change in net savings	$1,300	
Consumption	$43,700	Consuming less than you earn

decisions have on net worth. In table 3.4, you use a credit card to finance a few big-ticket items, such as a vacation, a new wardrobe for work, or attending a friend's wedding, that are not assets. You then use your net income to pay off a large part of the credit card balance. Because the amount of the credit card balance exceeds the net income you earned that year, your debts increase, and your net worth declines.

If you rely less on your credit card during the year, you might use the net income to pay off the entire credit card balance (table 3.5). Moreover, you will also have money left over to supplement your savings. In this scenario, your net worth rises.

It is particularly important to analyze your cash flow, which includes looking at your income, recurring expenses, savings and debts, before making a big change, such as moving to a new apartment, buying a condo, getting married, or starting a business. Analyze both your current situation and the revisions you need to make considering the changes on the horizon.

Establish Priorities

After you analyze your income, expenses, and cash flow, you can identify ways to save more money and grow your net income. You can also make a goal of saving and investing a fixed dollar amount every month. Automatic savings plans, which you can use to save for a down payment, graduate school, or retirement, are a relatively painless way to save. You can set up an automatic transfer from your bank on the day you get paid. This is called "paying yourself first." Part 4 of this book elaborates on the benefits of consistency in savings and investing.

Investing a fixed-dollar amount at set intervals is called **dollar-cost averaging**. An advantage of automatic savings plans is that you invest the same dollar amount every time. When markets are weak, or asset values have fallen, the same dollar amount will allow you to buy more shares of a mutual fund or a stock than when markets are strong and investable assets have appreciated. In this example, the average cost of your investment will be lower than if you decide to buy a set number of shares periodically.

. . . .

When we got married, my husband worked at a mutual fund company. For years, he transferred money every month from his checking account into a few of the mutual funds managed by his company. With dollar-cost averaging, he bought more shares when markets were weaker and shares were less expensive. When markets were strong, he bought fewer shares. Making this commitment to invest every month was a relatively painless way to save for our first down payment.

. . . .

CHAPTER 4

Analyze Your Risk

*T*HE NEXT TASK IN analyzing your financial profile is to assess the risk associated with your financial life. You need to take a close and honest look at your finances, ask yourself some questions, and consider uncertainties and exposures. The steps in this chapter will help you analyze your situation in the same way that an objective third party would, highlighting areas that you might be able to change in order to reduce the financial risks in your life.

Step 1: Analyze Your Sources of Income

The first consideration is your income. Ask yourself these questions:

- Is your salary steady or variable?
- Do you rely on commissions or bonuses?
- Do you work in a cyclical industry?

If you answered "yes" to these questions, you should not carry a lot of debt. Likewise, you should make sure to have an ample cash reserve. Determining how large a cash reserve you need is covered in part 4.

Step 2: Evaluate Your Creditworthiness

Too much debt increases the riskiness of your financial profile. In this step, you will learn more about credit scores and some general principles to help you manage debt prudently.

MYFL Golden Rule 5
Building good credit is essential.

You can pay for large expenditures over time using student loans, mortgages, and car loans and leases, but how you handle these and other debts has a significant impact on your net worth. In addition, how you handle these debts plus credit cards and cellular and utility bills has a big impact on your credit score. Credit scores range from 300 to 850 (figure 4.1).

Not only does your credit score determine the interest rate you will be charged when you borrow money, it also determines whether or not you will be able to get credit if you need to borrow. Keep in mind that each lender has different requirements for a minimum credit score that they will approve for potential borrowers. Depending on the lender and the type of loan you are requesting, being in the "Good" range may not be "good enough."

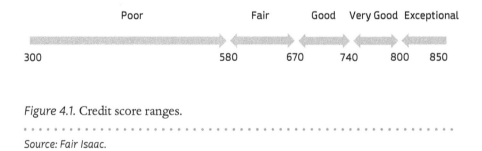

Figure 4.1. Credit score ranges.

Source: Fair Isaac.

The first step in evaluating your creditworthiness is to check your credit report, which includes your entire credit history. You can request a free credit report once a year at AnnualCreditReport.com. Report any errors immediately to the three credit bureaus—TransUnion, Equifax, and Experian. Some personal finance websites, including Credit Karma and Mint, will provide your credit score for free. To learn more about credit reports and credit scores, visit https://www.consumerfinance.gov or https://www.usa.gov/credit-reports.

When it comes to credit cards, less is always more—this adage applies to the number of cards as well as to the amount on them. Having too many credit card accounts hurts your credit score. In my opinion, it is wise to avoid cards issued by a retailer, also known as a store card. You might get some sort of benefit or discount when you open a store card account, but the act of opening the account has a negative impact on your credit score. If you want to reduce the number of credit cards you have, do not close more than one at a time. Closing a number of credit card accounts at one time will have a negative impact on your credit score. Before you do anything, check your credit report. Sometimes a store card that has not been used for a while has already been closed by the retailer.

Consumer Debts

When managing your financial life, remember that discipline has a big impact on your net worth. When you are thinking of buying a big item, think about whether you can actually afford the item, not just whether you can afford the payments. When you choose to finance a big item, you are adding a fixed obligation to your monthly expenses. What happens if your income goes down? You will have even less cushion and less flexibility than you currently do. Remember, if you borrow on your credit card to buy an item that is not an asset and is consumed—like a vacation—your net worth goes down. I love to travel and treasure my family vacations, but I do not use debt to pay for them. It is okay to use your credit card to pay for vacation expenses while you are away, as long as you make sure that you will be able to pay the balance in full upon your return.

Mortgages

Buying a home or condo and getting a mortgage are major milestones in your financial life that require careful consideration. Whether or not it is the right time to buy and how much you can afford depend on your particular situation and circumstances. This section has some general guidelines to help you decide.

- Do not buy a home or condo that costs more than 2.5 times your annual income.
- Mortgage interest, principal, taxes, real estate taxes, and insurance should not exceed 28 percent of your gross, or pretax, monthly income. This is called the **front-end ratio.**
- The combination of front-end ratio expenses plus all your other fixed obligations, such as car payments, credit card bills, student loans, alimony, and child support, should not exceed 36 percent of your gross, or pretax, monthly pay. This is called the **back-end ratio.**
- Don't buy a home or condo unless you expect to live there for several years. A lot of expenses are associated with moving. Not only are closing costs and movers expensive, but outlays for improvements, furniture, and decorating can really add up.

Mortgage bankers and brokers are paid to help you finance your home. They may use different debt-to-income guidelines than are appropriate for your comfort level. Just because you have been approved for a mortgage for a particular amount doesn't mean that you need or should have a mortgage of that size.

Home Equity Loans

As with any debt, home equity loans can get you into trouble if they are not managed carefully. It is prudent to be approved for a home equity line of credit before you need to use it. Get approved when you don't need the money, because your financial profile will likely be better than when you do need the money. If you are approved for a home equity loan when your personal finances are in very good shape, you will be considered a low credit risk. If your circumstances change and you wait until you need the money to be approved, your financial profile may not be as solid. At that point, your credit profile will likely be riskier, and you may be charged a higher interest rate, or you may not be approved.

Step 3: Have a Plan to Pay Off Debt

Always have a plan to reduce debt and always think in terms of net worth. All debt, even your mortgage, should be viewed as temporary. Your plan should be to pay off your mortgage by the time you think you will retire. If you are not certain that you will be able to do that, your mortgage is probably too large. If you have an occasional inflow, such as a bonus or a larger-than-expected tax refund, consider using some or all of it to pay down debt, especially credit card debt. Having a payoff plan, even for small debts, means that these obligations are less likely to become big worries. Part 4 will address how to manage multiple goals—both saving and paying down debt.

. . . .

After graduating from college, I borrowed money from my parents to help me get through the first few months. I worked a part-time job before starting a full-time position. I lived very modestly and kept a tally of what I owed my parents on a bulletin board. Seeing the size of the debt every day kept me on track. Once I started paying my parents back, seeing my progress toward paying the debt down was great motivation to continue to do so.

. . . .

Step 4: Examine Your Insurance Coverage

Insurance is a "must" in many areas of your life. You are required to have homeowner's insurance if you have a mortgage and to have auto insurance in most states if you drive. If you rent your home, you should have renter's insurance, even though it is not always required by landlords. Renters insurance is usually not expensive. If you live in a multiunit building, someone else's carelessness could have an impact on your apartment and your possessions. When you are just starting out, it may seem like you don't have much to insure. But imagine if there was a fire or flood in your apartment. Think about trying to replace everything—furniture, clothing, shoes, bedding, dishes, cookware, electronics, luggage. You get the picture.

Whether you own or rent your home, take pictures or videos of your possessions and store the images in a safe place. An ideal spot is on a thumb drive, with your vital papers in a safety deposit or fire-safe box, or in the cloud using a secure cloud provider.

Don't forget to consider life and disability insurance when you analyze your risk profile. If you have a family, both are important. In my opinion, term life insurance is usually more appropriate than whole life insurance. Whole life insurance provides coverage for your lifetime. With a whole life policy, there is certainty that you will die and that your beneficiaries will collect, and that certainty is reflected in the cost of the policy. Term life policies provide coverage for only a term, or for a certain period of time. Term life insurance is less expensive than whole life insurance because there is no certainty that you will die during the term of your policy. If you are married with a family, you can choose a policy term and amount that covers your family when your children are young and provides enough to get your children through college and into their working years.

For those who have studied statistics, remember that probability is a central component of assessing risk. For young people, the probability of becoming disabled is much higher than the probability of death. Therefore, disability insurance is a good idea, especially for young families.

Life insurance agents often market life insurance as an investment. I am not a fan of insurance as an investment. Insurance carries fees, restrictions, and commissions. My advice is to use insurance to protect yourself from big risks and to use investments to grow your money. Both insurance and investments have a place in your financial toolkit.

Step 5: Consider Other Risks and Exposures

Advances in technology and mobile communication have changed the way we manage our finances. These innovations save time and allow us to be more informed consumers. But the innovations have also introduced new risks and exposures.

Identity Theft and Fraud

Review your credit report regularly. You are entitled to a free credit report once a year. You can download your free report and search for errors or indications of fraud at www.annualcreditreport.com.

If you will not be in the market for a new loan soon, it is possible to freeze or lock your credit profile to reduce the chance of identity theft. In that case, you need to contact each of the three credit bureaus: Equifax, Experian, and TransUnion. Depending on what state you live in, there may be a fee to freeze your profile and another fee to unfreeze your profile. The fee is often waived if you have been the victim of identity theft.

If you receive a suspicious email, text, or voicemail that appears to come from your credit card company, do not respond. These communications can appear official but are often from hackers. If you are ever unsure about communications from your credit card company, call the number on the back of your card.

. . . .

When I was speaking at an event, I discussed the benefits of diversifying investments across different asset classes. One of the guests asked whether having multiple credit cards would reduce the likelihood of identity theft because, with multiple cards, she was not putting all her eggs in one basket. I responded that having a number of credit cards increases her odds for identity theft—there are more cards to keep track of and more opportunities for a hacker to access her credit information, not to mention the detrimental impact on her credit score and her net worth.

. . . .

Privacy

Be careful about what information you share online. For your online accounts, never provide a financial services company more information than necessary. Most financial firms ask you to link other accounts with other financial firms on their website. A firm may suggest that aggregating account information from other firms on their site will give you a more comprehensive view of your financial profile. Be very careful. I am concerned about the security of sharing all of your financial accounts and information on a financial company's website. The asset allocation grid in chapter 3 is a better option.

Financial firms want to know as much about you as possible for marketing purposes. Some online financial management or budgeting tools may ask you to link your investment account to a site, which also makes me nervous. These tools can be very helpful for tracking your spending and setting up automatic savings plans, but it is not necessary to link your investment account(s). Moreover, investment firms may advertise on a financial management site, and some of these firms are offered as recommended providers. This also makes me uncomfortable. The savings apps tend to pay very low rates on savings. You will be able to earn a higher return in your investment account. It is easy to transfer funds accumulated from an automated savings app to an investment account.

Technological Risks

Given the amount of sensitive information traveling through your computer and mobile devices every day, you need to protect your data and limit access to it. Install updates regularly because they can provide the most current defense against viruses and malware.

Although it is obvious—and good common sense—be very careful using open networks. Access your financial accounts only from a secure network. With time, your financial accounts will grow, and so will the potential losses from hacks.

There are many ways to enhance the security of your passwords. As tempting as it is, do not use the same password for everything. Create a variety of passwords with a mix of upper- and lowercase letters, symbols, and numbers. Use a pass phrase rather than a password. A pass phrase is longer and includes more characters than a password. The more characters in your password or pass phrase, the harder it is for someone to figure it out.

Consider using a password management service to keep your passwords organized and secure. I have found that it is far easier to remember one master password or pass phrase than a unique password for every site. Password management services often flag passwords that are too simple and therefore not secure. Some will even generate passwords for you.

A handwritten list of passwords can be secure, as long as you keep the list in a safe place away from your computer. Whatever method you decide to use, never instruct your browser or a website to remember a password. If your laptop is stolen and your passwords are saved in a browser, someone will be able to gain access to your accounts easily.

A friend saved a copy of her tax return on her laptop's hard drive. The laptop was stolen. Think of all the information contained on your tax return. Pretty scary. . . .

Risk Management versus Risk Tolerance

When you analyze risks to your financial profile, you need to be objective and consider how another person would view your financial situation. Be honest with yourself so you can identify areas where you might be able to make changes and alter the risk associated with your finances. This is known as **risk management**.

In contrast to risk management, **risk tolerance** is about personal preferences. It is about how comfortable you are taking on risk. The riskiness of different investment choices varies. The next part of this book covers fundamental investing concepts, types of investments, and types of investment accounts. Just as you need to be honest and objective about the riskiness of your financial profile, you need to be honest and objective about your comfort level with different degrees of volatility, or risk. As you consider if you want to be conservative, moderate, or aggressive with your investments, think about your time horizon. Think about liquidity. Last, and perhaps most important, talk with your partner if you have one. No two people are exactly alike. When it comes to your family's finances, you and your partner should be on the same page.

PART 3

Educate Yourself About Investing

The secret of getting ahead is getting started.

—MARK TWAIN

In this section, we cover investing concepts, asset classes, and types of investments and accounts. As you read through these chapters, remember that not all investable assets or accounts will be appropriate for you. Each investor's needs and goals are unique.

CHAPTER 5

Some Fundamental Concepts

To UNDERSTAND INVESTING, you must know about some fundamental concepts. These concepts will help you become a more informed and successful investor. Some have been

Investable Assets *What to Invest In*	Investment Structures *Ways to Invest*	Investment Accounts *Why to Invest*
• Cash and money market • Bonds • Stocks • Derivatives • Master limited partnerships (MLPs) • Real estate investment trusts (REITs) • Private capital • Alternative assets • Commodities and currencies	• Individual account • Mutual funds • Index funds • Exchange traded funds (ETFs) • Exchange traded notes (ETNs) • Target date funds	• Taxable • 401(k)s and 403(b)s • Individual retirement accounts (IRAs) • Roth IRA and 401(k)s • Annuities • 529 plans

Fundamental Investing Concepts

Figure 5.1. Fundamental investing concepts.

introduced already; others will be new. These fundamental concepts will provide a foundation for understanding investments, markets, and investment strategies. After you become familiar with some fundamental investing concepts, you will be ready to explore different types of investable assets (such as stocks, or equities, and bonds), different types of investment structures (such as mutual funds and ETFs), and different types of investment accounts (such as 401(k)s and IRAs).

Supply and Demand

Supply and **demand** play a central role in investing. The value of an item depends not on what you paid for it, but on what someone else would be willing to pay for it today. Four principles are tied to supply and demand, as demonstrated in table 5.1.

TABLE 5.1. Supply and demand.			
Supply and demand: Four principles			
If . . . And . . .		Then	Example
There is a fixed supply of something			
	Demand increases	Price will rise	After an artist dies, the prices of existing works go up.
	Demand decreases	Price will decline	A retailer cuts the price of an out-of-style item to move inventory.
There is a fixed demand for something			
	Supply increases	Price will decline	When a fad is overproduced and is widely available, retailers will have to cut prices.
	Supply decreases	Price will rise	The prices of agricultural products rise following a drought.

Yield, Total Return, and Compounding

For any asset, **yield** is the income earned divided by the price of the asset, such as a bond or a share of stock. Price and yield move in opposite directions, a concept that can be a little confusing. If the price of an asset goes down, then the yield goes up. If the price of an asset rises, then the yield declines. Let's walk through the math.

- If a $1,000 bond earns 5 percent interest, it earns $50 on a $1,000 asset, or $50 divided by $1,000, which is a 5 percent yield. If the price of the bond increases to $1,050, the yield declines to $50 on a $1,050 asset, or 4.8 percent. The income for a bond is fixed, so changes in yield are always driven by changes in the demand for—and market price of—a particular bond.

  $50 ÷ $1,000 = 5.0% and 50 ÷ $1,050 = 4.8%

- If a share of stock is worth $50 and pays a $1 dividend per share, the yield is $1 divided by $50, or 2 percent. Stock yields fluctuate depending on the demand for—and market price of—a particular stock. If the stock declines in value to $45, then the yield increases to 2.2 percent. If a company increases its dividend, then the yield will also change. Raising the dividend to $1.10 results in a 2.2 percent yield.

  $1 ÷ $50 = 2.0% and 1 ÷ $45 = 2.2% and 1.10 ÷ $50 = 2.2%

Total return is the combination of yield and the change in valuation. Total return takes into account the income earned on an investment, such as interest or dividends, and any appreciation or depreciation in the value of the asset. If a stock earns a 2 percent dividend yield and appreciates 5 percent in a year, the total return is 7 percent.

  2% dividend yield + 5% appreciation = 7% total return

Compounding means that there is growth on the growth. The compounding of returns has a significant impact on the value of investments over time. For example, an investment of $100 with appreciation of 7 percent will be worth $107 at the end of the first year. If the investment appreciates 7 percent again in the second year, the return would be 7 percent on $107, or $7.49. At the end of the second year, the investment would be worth $107 plus $7.49, or $114.49. In the second year, the increase in the value of the investment of $7.49 is greater than the increase in year 1 of $7.00 because of the growth on the growth.

7% growth on $100 = $107 and 7% growth on $107 = $114.49

Risk

In the investing world, **risk** is the variability, or volatility, of investment returns. **Volatility** is measured by the dispersion, or the standard deviation, of outcomes, or returns. The **standard deviation** is how far an actual return might be from the average, or expected, return for a particular investment. With investments, the greater the standard deviation, the greater the risk.

The weather is a good illustration of standard deviation. A forecast gives an average, or expected, temperature for a city on a particular day of the year. In some regions, such as Southern California, there is less variability, or volatility, in temperature for a particular day of the year. In other areas, such as Chicago, there is much more variability, or volatility, in temperature for a particular day of the year. Thus, the standard deviation in weather for a particular day of the year is greater in Chicago than it is in Southern California.

Investors are compensated for taking risk. In other words, as risk or volatility rises, so should the anticipated return. Volatility, or the standard deviation of returns, varies depending on

> ## Sell in May and Go Away
>
> Historically, the level of trading activity, or volume, in the
> stock market declines during the summer months compared
> with the rest of the year. Reduced trading volume can
> sometimes lead to greater volatility in stock prices. In some
> years, the market has not performed well during the summer
> months. Thus the adage "Sell in May and go away," suggesting
> that investors should sell investments in May and sit on cash
> throughout the summer. This is not, however, a recommended
> strategy. You should not try to move in and out of the market,
> or **time the market**. Rather, you should have a long-term
> orientation. That said, be careful not to buy or sell during any
> period with significantly lower trading activity. There can be
> greater volatility on a slow trading day, such as the day before
> a holiday or the Friday after Thanksgiving.

the type of investment. It also depends on the amount of trading activity for that asset. If there is less trading activity, or trading volume, volatility will increase.

If you are investing in mutual funds, it is helpful to look at the standard deviation for each of your choices. Comparing standard deviations gives you a sense of the relative riskiness of each option. This information is available on Morningstar.com. If you want to do in-depth research on funds or any other investments and have a library card, you can usually access Morningstar and other investment resources for free at your local public library.

Liquidity

Liquidity reflects how easily an asset can be converted to cash. In general, assets such as stocks and bonds are liquid. College savings plans and retirement savings accounts may hold liquid

Bullish or Bearish

The terms *bullish* and *bearish* are used to describe an outlook for financial markets. A bull thrusts his horns up when he does battle. A bear swings his or her arms down in a fight. If you are bullish, you think that the market will rise. The term *bull market* is often used to describe a continuous period of rising values. If you are bearish, you think that the market will go down. A *correction* is often used to describe a decline of 10 percent or more in the market. Some investors refer to a decline of more than 20 percent as a *bear market*. Investors often track the amount of time since the last correction and since the last bear market.

investments, but the accounts themselves are less liquid than other types of investment accounts because there are penalties for withdrawing money early. Real estate assets are normally classified as illiquid—you cannot necessarily sell your home at any given time.

Assets that are less liquid can decline in value significantly during a financial crisis. During periods of economic turmoil, illiquid assets, such as homes or condos, can become even more illiquid. When many people are selling assets, whether it is a stock or a home, illiquidity makes the situation more challenging. In a financial crisis, investors may have to sell what they can rather than selling lower-quality assets that they should.

Do not plan to use investable assets that are illiquid or could fluctuate in value to pay for large obligations like tuition or taxes that are due soon. Rather, fund these near-term obligations with the most liquid, least volatile assets that you have access to, such as cash or money market funds.

Concentration and Diversification

The saying "Don't put all your eggs in one basket" applies to investments, because concentration increases risk. Whether you invest your money yourself or work with a professional, never put all your assets in the same basket—the same kind of stock, bond, mutual fund, or other investment.

In addition to avoiding concentration, diversification is key to improving investment results. Various asset classes, or types of investments, tend to perform differently under certain market conditions—some perform better, and some perform worse, depending on what is going on with the economy and financial markets. The best investment strategy is to have a diverse portfolio that includes a mixture of stocks, bonds, and international investments.

Diversification across asset classes helps reduce risk; correlation illustrates this benefit. **Correlation** measures how things, such as investment returns, move in relation to each other. Some asset class returns are more correlated than others. Say you invest in a stock and in a bond. If the economy picks up steam, corporate earnings will likely rise and so will your stock. As the economy picks up steam, however, the Federal Reserve may raise interest rates to keep inflation in check. When the Federal Reserve raises rates, the value of the bond that you hold will decline. Another investor could get a higher interest rate on a new bond issued today because rates are now higher in the market. The decline in the value of your bond is offset to some degree by the increase in the value of your stock. Hence the benefit of diversification.

Not only should you diversify across asset classes, you should diversify within asset classes. Invest in different types of stocks and different types of bonds. An easy way to diversify is to invest in companies that are different sizes. **Capitalization**, or cap, is the market value of all shares of stock outstanding. There are small-cap, mid-cap, and large-cap stocks. Here are some general definitions:

- Small-cap companies have market valuations of less than $2 billion to $3 billion, and microcap companies have even smaller market valuations of less than $500 million.
- Large-cap companies are usually market valuations of greater than $10 billion to $15 billion. Megacap

companies are even larger and have market valuations of greater than $50 billion to $100 billion.

- Midcap companies fall between large and small caps.

Changes in the economy and changes in the financial markets can have different impacts on large-cap stocks than on small-cap stocks. Therefore, diversifying across market capitalization ranges lowers the risk of your investment profile (figure 5.2).

Figure 5.2. Stock market capitalization ranges.

Fees

The impact of fees over the life of an investment or the life of an investment account can be significant, so an understanding of fees is essential. In the investment arena, fees are usually charged as a percentage of assets. They are often quoted in terms of basis points. A **basis point** is one one-hundredth of 1 percent, or 0.01 percent. In other words, 100 basis points equals 1.0 percent, and 50 basis points equals one-half of 1 percent, or 0.50 percent.

MYFL Golden Rule 6

You should know the all-in fees for any investment that you make.

There are many kinds of fees. Some fees are transaction based: these are paid to brokers as compensation for putting clients in an investment or for executing a trade. Examples of transaction-based fees are commissions and sales loads. With a **commission**, the brokerage firm charges a fee for each transaction. A **sales load** is a one-time front-end or back-end fee that is paid to the brokerage firm selling you a mutual fund. A front-end load is a reduction to the initial investment. If you make a $100 investment with a 5 percent sales load, you are putting only $95 to work; $5 of that $100 goes to the brokerage firm. A back-end load is a reduction of proceeds. If you sell a $100 investment with a 5 percent back-end load, you receive $95. Not all mutual funds have sales loads. Discount and online brokerage firms offer a large number of no-load funds.

In contrast to brokers, who charge commissions and loads, fee-based advisers are paid an annual fee based on a percentage of assets under management. The adviser is not paid to execute trades. Rather, he or she is paid to invest your money. If the investments perform well, the portfolio grows, and the financial adviser also does well. Unlike brokers, who charge transaction-based fees, incentives are aligned for fee-based financial advisers and their clients. Advisory fees traditionally average around 1 percent, and often range from 0.75 percent up to 1.75 percent. For larger accounts, fees may be lower. Competition from online financial planning models has helped bring down fees.

For mutual funds, the management fee depends on the type of fund. According to the Investment Company Institute, Lipper, and Morningstar, the average annual stock fund management fee in 2016 was 63 basis points. For bond funds, the average annual management fee was 51 basis points. Management fees have been coming down. Twenty years ago, the average fee was 104 basis points for stock funds and 84 basis points for bonds funds.[5]

Compared with the averages just mentioned, fees are higher for smaller cap funds and international funds. Researching small-cap and international stocks tends to be more expensive than researching large-cap US-based stocks. Traveling to meet management, learning about products, and speaking with customers can be challenging if the company is not easily accessible or if little is known about the company. Some small-company and international stocks are **below the radar**, or not well-known by most investors. This can be a good thing if the fund finds hidden gems that are undervalued.

Fees are lower for index funds and for exchange-traded funds, or ETFs. Depending on the type of index fund or ETF, the fee may be less than 10 basis points. More specialized index funds have a slightly higher fee. These types of investments are covered in greater detail in chapter 7.

Table 5.2 illustrates the long-term impact of fees. For example, $1,000 earning a 7 percent return will grow to $4,322 after thirty years if the investment is in a fund charging 2 percent. That same $1,000 earning 7 percent would grow to $6,614 after thirty years if the fund charged only 0.50 percent.

Although investment fees may seem complicated, they are important to understand because of their impact on the growth of your money. If you meet with a prospective financial adviser, fees should be an essential part of the discussion. In a mutual fund prospectus, fees are noted in the table of contents. Fees are also listed on Morningstar, online brokerage firms' websites, and the various mutual fund marketplaces. Make sure you understand all fees, whether you invest on your own or through a broker or adviser.

Tax Efficiency

As an investor, you need to consider the impact of taxes. The taxes owed on an investment depend on the type of investment account

TABLE 5.2. Long-term impact of fees on an investment.

Annual investment return	7.0%		
Initial investment	$1,000		
	Year-end balance at different fee rates		
Year	2.0%	1.0%	0.5%
1	$1,050	$1,060	$1,065
2	$1,103	$1,124	$1,134
3	$1,158	$1,191	$1,208
4	$1,216	$1,262	$1,286
5	$1,276	$1,338	$1,370
6	$1,340	$1,419	$1,459
7	$1,407	$1,504	$1,554
8	$1,477	$1,594	$1,655
9	$1,551	$1,689	$1,763
10	$1,629	$1,791	$1,877
11	$1,710	$1,898	$1,999
12	$1,796	$2,012	$2,129
13	$1,886	$2,133	$2,267
14	$1,980	$2,261	$2,415
15	$2,079	$2,397	$2,572
16	$2,183	$2,540	$2,739
17	$2,292	$2,693	$2,917
18	$2,407	$2,854	$3,107
19	$2,527	$3,026	$3,309
20	$2,653	$3,207	$3,524
21	$2,786	$3,400	$3,753
22	$2,925	$3,604	$3,997
23	$3,072	$3,820	$4,256
24	$3,225	$4,049	$4,533
25	$3,386	$4,292	$4,828
26	$3,556	$4,549	$5,141
27	$3,733	$4,822	$5,476
28	$3,920	$5,112	$5,832
29	$4,116	$5,418	$6,211
30	$4,322	$5,743	$6,614
Difference		$1,421	$2,292

Note: Assumes that the initial investment was made at the beginning of the year.

that is holding the investment. For **tax-deferred** accounts, such as 401(k)s and 403(b)s, you contribute money from your paycheck before it is taxed, known as "pre-tax dollars." In other words, you do not pay taxes on the portion of your salary that goes directly into your 401(k) or 403(b). Moreover, you do not pay taxes on the income or capital gains generated each year. Instead, you pay taxes when you withdraw money from the account. Roth IRAs and college savings plans, such as 529s, are examples of a **tax-advantaged** account. You fund these kinds of accounts with after-tax dollars and you do not get a tax break up front. After you fund a Roth IRA or 529, the income, appreciation, and withdrawals are tax free.

For **taxable accounts**, income and capital gains are not tax exempt or tax deferred, so you owe taxes each year. Tax efficiency means that you are managing a taxable account in a way that minimizes the taxes owed each year. For any investment, the tax treatment for the income and gains depends on a number of factors.

Capital Gains and Losses

A **capital gain** or **capital loss** is the difference between the cost basis of an investment and what is received when the investment is sold. Remember that the cost basis is the original amount paid for an investment plus or minus any adjustments to the original cost that occur while you hold the investment.

For assets that have appreciated, you pay taxes on capital gains when you sell the asset. There are some important considerations to keep in mind with respect to taxes on investment gains and losses. Short-term capital gains occur when an appreciated investment is held for one year or less. Long-term gains occur when an appreciated investment is held for at least one year plus one day. Tax rates for short-term gains are much higher than they are for long-term gains. Short-term gains are taxed as ordinary income at a rate that can be as high as 37 percent, depending on your tax bracket. **Ordinary income** is the tax rate that you pay on your wages or salary and on interest and other sources of income. Depending on where you live, state taxes may also apply.

Investors who have taxable income above a certain amount also pay a **net investment income tax**, or **NIIT**, of 3.8 percent, for a total rate as high as 40.8 percent. The rate for long-term gains can be as high as 23.8 percent, or 20 percent plus 3.8 percent with the NIIT.

When investors take, or **realize**, a loss on an investment, they can use that loss to offset some or all of the capital gains they have realized on other investments. As an investor, you should keep track of gains and losses as you incur them and try to offset your gains with losses, especially as year-end draws near. It is also possible to carry losses forward to offset gains in the future. The amount of losses that you can carry over each year, however, is limited. You cannot realize a capital loss in the event of a **wash sale**, which occurs when an investor sells an investment to realize a loss and buys it back within thirty days.

Taxes on Dividends

For taxable accounts, the treatment of dividends depends on whether they are **qualified** or **nonqualified**. Most US company dividends are qualified and are taxed at the same rate as long-term capital gains. Depending on your income, these rates can be as high as 20.0 percent. Dividends from foreign companies and REITs (real estate investment trusts) are nonqualified. Investment income from nonqualified sources is taxed at the ordinary income rate, which can be as high as 37 percent.

If you do not rely on income from your investments to help you live day-to-day, you should focus on investments that appreciate in value, rather than those that generate interest and dividends. For investments that generate interest and dividends, also called **current income**, you will pay taxes each year. With appreciated securities, you decide when you want to sell and pay capital gains.

CHAPTER 6

Investable Assets: What to Invest In

Now that you are familiar with some fundamental concepts involved in investing, let's delve into the various asset classes—how they work, what affects their value, and the types of investments that are available.

Investable Assets *What to Invest In*	Investment Structures *Ways to Invest*	Investment Accounts *Why to Invest*
• Cash and money market • Bonds • Stocks • Derivatives • Master limited partnerships (MLPs) • Real estate investment trusts (REITs) • Private capital • Alternative assets • Commodities and currencies	• Individual account • Mutual funds • Index funds • Exchange traded funds (ETFs) • Exchange traded notes (ETNs) • Target date funds	• Taxable • 401(k)s and 403(b)s • Individual retirement accounts (IRAs) • Roth IRA and 401(k)s • Annuities • 529 plans

Fundamental Investing Concepts

Figure 6.1. Investable assets.

FDIC *Insurance:* *What Is Covered, What Is Not?*

As of this writing, FDIC insurance coverage is limited to $250,000 per account. The limits depend on the type of account— whether it is a joint account or an individual account. The FDIC does not cover securities, such as stocks, bonds, money market funds, annuities, or mutual funds, even if they are offered by a bank. Visit www.fdic.gov to learn more.

(Note: if you use an automated savings app, make sure any funds are deposited into an FDIC-insured account.)

The Capital Markets

Before we discuss asset classes, let's begin with the **capital markets**, commonly referred to as the financial markets. Investors provide money, or **capital**, to companies, governments, and municipalities. In exchange for providing money, or capital, investors expect to earn a return. Companies, governments, and municipalities use capital for a variety of reasons. For example, a company may use short-term capital to finance short-term needs, such as inventory or accounts receivable. A municipality may use long-term capital to fund longer-term needs, such as buildings, equipment, and infrastructure such as roads or bridges.

Let's look at how a company raises capital. Companies can raise money by **issuing debt** (i.e., selling bonds to investors) or by **issuing equity** (i.e., selling stock). A key distinction between the two methods of raising capital is that a bond is an obligation, or debt; stock, or equity, represents ownership. Bondholders have priority over, or are senior to, equity shareholders. In other words, if a company is in financial distress, bondholders will be paid before shareholders.

The capital markets encompass both the primary market and the secondary market. When companies issue new stock or new bonds to raise capital, the stock or bonds are sold in the **primary market**. In an **initial public offering**, or **IPO**, investors buy stock or bonds from the company, or issuer. After an initial public offering, investors buy or sell stock and bonds from each other. This is called the **secondary market**. Trading—buying and selling securities—takes place on **exchanges**. The capital markets are interconnected around the globe.

When a company issues stock or bonds in the primary market, some investors may choose to hang on to their stock or bonds, and others may choose to sell their stock or bonds to other investors in the secondary market. As investors begin buying or selling stock and bonds in the secondary market, the value of what people hold changes. Remember the fundamental concept that the value of what you own does not depend on what you paid for it, but rather on what someone else is willing to pay for it today.

There are two main types of investors in the capital markets. **Retail investors** are individuals who act on their own behalf. When you invest your savings, either by yourself or with a broker or financial adviser, you are considered a retail investor. **Institutional investors** manage money for others. Examples of institutional investors are mutual funds, insurance companies, endowments, foundations, and pension plans.

Common Types of Investable Assets

Now that you have had a brief introduction to the capital markets, let's take a look at different types of investable assets, how they work, and what causes them to increase or decrease in value. We'll start with the most commonly held investable assets.

Cash and Money Market Funds

The most liquid asset is cash in a checking or savings account. You can access cash from an ATM twenty-four hours a day, seven days a week. Banks also offer **certificates of deposit**, or **CDs**, as an alternative to savings accounts. Like savings accounts, CDs are insured by the Federal Deposit Insurance Company, or FDIC.

With a checking or savings account, you have total control over your money; with a CD, the bank has the use of your money for a specific amount of time. You can withdraw your money before the end of the CD's term, but there is a penalty. Banks also offer **money market deposit accounts** that are FDIC insured. These accounts are like savings accounts, but they allow you to write checks. There is usually a limit to the number of transactions allowed over a period of time.

Money market funds invest in high-quality, very short-term, liquid securities like short-term government debt, CDs, and short-term municipal bonds. Unlike money market deposit accounts, money market funds are not FDIC insured.

Bonds

When you invest in a bond, you are loaning money to an entity, or an **issuer**, for a specific amount of time. The various types of issuers include companies, municipalities, the US government, and foreign governments. Remember that bonds pay investors interest at a fixed amount, which is why bonds are also known as **fixed-income securities**.

The two components of bonds are principal and interest. **Principal** is the face value of the bond, and it is the amount returned to you when the bond matures. **Interest** on the principal is paid periodically, usually semiannually, over the life, or **term**, of the bond. At the end of the term, or when the bond matures, the issuer pays the final interest payment and returns the principal.

For example, if you invest in a $1,000 face value bond with a five-year term and 4 percent interest payable semiannually, you will receive an interest payment of $20 every six months for five years. At the end of the five-year term, you will also receive $1,000—the face value of the bond—along with the final interest payment of $20.

FACTORS THAT AFFECT A BOND'S VALUE

Bonds are valued based on the expected receipt of interest payments and principal over the term of the bond and the relative riskiness of that stream of payments. Changes at the company, in the financial markets, and in the US and foreign economies all can affect a bond's value. Over time, as bonds trade in the secondary market, the value increases or decreases depending on the creditworthiness, or credit quality, of the issuer and current economic and market conditions. If a bond trades at face value, it is at **par**. Bonds can also trade at a premium or a discount to par.

> ### Coupons
>
> Interest payments are sometimes called **coupons.** In the old days, investors pulled a coupon off a bond and submitted it to the issuer to collect an interest payment. Interest payments are now paid electronically, but you might still hear the word "coupon" used.

Credit risk. A change in the creditworthiness of the issuer (positive or negative) will affect a bond's value. If the issuer, such as a company or government entity, becomes less creditworthy, the bond declines in value. If a company's financial condition deteriorates to the point where the issuer stops paying interest (or principal), it is in default.

To issue debt, an issuer needs a **credit rating**. Rating agencies conduct an independent analysis of the issuer and assign a credit rating. To indicate a top rating, S&P and Fitch use AAA, or "triple A," and Moody's uses Aaa. The top rating is followed by AA (or "double A"), A (or "single A"), BBB, BB, B, CCC, CC, C, and then D. There are also distinctions such as "plus," or +, and "minus," or –. For example, AAA is followed by AA+, and then AA, and then AA–, and so on.

The higher the credit rating, the lower the perceived credit risk. The lower the credit risk, the lower the interest rate that an issuer needs to pay investors. AAA ratings are rare. Very few companies and approximately a dozen countries have a AAA rating. In the US, only two companies—Johnson & Johnson and Microsoft— have AAA ratings. US government debt is currently rated AA+. Any bond rated BB or lower is considered noninvestment grade. These are also referred to as **speculative**, or **junk, bonds**.

With any asset class, investors should be compensated for taking on greater risk. With a higher risk asset, investors expect a greater return. With bonds, the spread is a measure of the relative riskiness. Bond prices are based on, or quoted, as a spread over Treasury bonds, or Treasuries. **Treasuries** are very low-risk investments and are backed by the full faith and credit of the United States. Bond spreads reflect risk. The difference between the yield on a bond and the interest rate for a Treasury bond with the same maturity is the **spread**.

bond yield – Treasury bond yield = spread

The riskier the credit, the wider the spread. For example, if a ten-year Treasury bond is trading at 3 percent and a ten-year corporate bond is trading at 6 percent, the spread is 3 percent, or 300 basis points. For a less-risky issuer with a higher credit rating, the yield on a ten-year bond might be 5.5 percent, or a spread of 2.5 percent, or 250 basis points. Spreads across the board can vary depending on how optimistic investors are about the future. If investors have a positive economic outlook, spreads will tend to be narrower. If investors are more pessimistic, bond spreads will widen.

Interest rate risk. Interest rates are determined by how much money is needed to compensate someone for borrowing his or her money. Interest rates also factor in expectations about inflation. If the expectation is for fast economic growth, interest rates will likely increase. If the growth rate of the US economy accelerates, the Federal Reserve is more likely to raise rates to keep inflation in check. With higher inflation, the dollars received back are worth less. Therefore, during an inflationary period, investors demand higher rates.

Remember that the value or price of an asset and yield move in opposite directions. If the value of a bond declines, the yield will rise. If the value of a bond rises, the yield will decline.

If interest rates rise after you invest in a bond, the bond's value will decline. Because an investor could get a higher interest rate in the market for a new bond, demand for your bond will go down, and your bond will trade at a discount. Likewise, if an issuer becomes less creditworthy after you invest, or if the rating agencies downgrade the issuer's credit rating, the bond will be worth less. The credit risk has increased, and other investors are not willing to pay as much as you did for the bond. If demand for the bond declines, due to higher interest rates available in the market or to declining credit quality, the value of the bond will decline, and the yield will increase. If a $1,000 bond's value drops to $950, the yield will increase to $50 on $950, or 5.3 percent.

If Market Interest Rates	Or Credit Quality	A Bond's Value	A Bond's Yield
Decrease	Improves	Rises	Declines
Increase	Deteriorates	Declines	Rises

Figure 6.2.

Duration measures how a bond's price is affected by a change in interest rates. Duration depends on the timing of the two types of payments received from a bond: interest payments, and the principal payment at maturity. Duration is expressed in years.

You could have two bonds with the same face value, or principal amount, and interest rates but with different maturities. All other things equal, a longer term until maturity will mean a longer duration. More of the cash flow is received by the bondholder later in the term compared to a bond with a shorter maturity.

If two bonds have the same face value and the same term, the one with the higher interest rate will have the shorter duration. In this case, you would receive more of the cash stream sooner than you would with the bond that has the lower stated interest rate and smaller periodic interest payments.

Understanding duration is key because duration determines volatility. The shorter the duration, the lower the interest rate volatility. The longer the duration, the greater the interest rate volatility. If you think interest rates will rise, invest in shorter-duration bonds rather than in longer-duration bonds. In a rising rate environment, a bond with a longer maturity will decline in value more than a shorter-maturity bond will. Longer duration is not always a bad thing, however. If you expect interest rates to drop, invest in longer-duration bonds. If you already own a bond that is paying a higher interest rate than is available for new bonds, you will receive a greater number of higher-than-market interest payments.

Duration helps to approximate the fluctuations in a bond's value in a rising or declining interest rate environment. As an illustration, if a bond has a duration of five years and rates increase by 1 percent, the value of the bond should decline by 5 x 1.0 percent, or 5 percent. For the same bond, a 1 percent decline in rates should increase the value of the bond by 5 x 1.0 percent, or 5 percent.

TYPES OF BONDS

There are different types of bonds, and the type of bond depends on the type of issuer. **Corporate bonds**, or **corporates**, are issued by companies. Bonds issued by companies based in the United States are called **domestic bonds**. In addition to credit risk and interest rate risk, the value of bonds issued by international companies is driven by changes in the value of the currency.

Here's an illustration of the impact of currency fluctuations on an international investment. If you are a US citizen and you invest in a corporate bond issued by a company based in Germany, the company, or issuer, will pay you interest in euros. If the euro strengthens, or appreciates, relative to the dollar, €1 costs more relative to $1. When you receive your interest payment in euros and convert them to dollars, you will receive more dollars than you would have if the euro had not appreciated. In contrast, if the euro weakens relative to the dollar, the interest payments in euros will be worth less in dollars.

Treasuries include all types and maturities of debt issued by the federal government. **Treasury bills** have maturities of less than one year, **Treasury notes** have maturities of between one and ten years, and **Treasury bonds** have maturities of ten years or longer. Interest on Treasury bills, notes, and bonds is exempt from state and local taxes. Interest on Treasury bills, notes, and bonds is not exempt from federal taxes.

Municipal bonds are issued by states or local governments, and there are two types. **General obligation** bonds represent general debts of a municipality. **Revenue** bonds are issued to fund a municipal project and use revenue tied to a specific source of income, such as a toll road, to make interest payments. Interest earned on most municipal bonds is exempt from federal taxation and from state and local taxation if the investor resides in the locale that issued the bond. If you invest in a municipal bond mutual fund, interest is not tax exempt. We will discuss mutual funds in the next chapter.

Sovereign bonds are issued by foreign governments. As with international corporate bonds, currency fluctuations can have an impact on sovereign bond returns.

Equity, or Stock

Equity represents ownership. When a company issues equity, or **stock,** to raise capital, investors buy a piece of that company and are entitled to a share of the company's earnings.

Remember that bondholders are senior to equity shareholders, or have priority. If a company is in financial distress, interest and principal are paid to bondholders before anything is paid to shareholders. This is an important distinction in a bankruptcy.

What Affects Value

Investment returns and the volatility of returns have an impact on the value of a stock and are the result of both market-specific and company-specific factors. Market-specific factors, such as the domestic economic outlook, politics, changes in US tax policy, and international forces, all have an impact on the value of equities. Company-specific factors include product launches, competitive advantages, competitive threats, and changes in management. If a company's earnings rise or fall, the value of the stock rises or falls. If expectations about the company's future earnings become better or worse, the stock rises or falls.

How a stock—or portfolio of stocks—performs relative to the overall market is a measure of volatility. Analyzing beta is one way to look at the expected investment performance of a stock. **Beta** indicates how a stock tends to perform relative to the overall market and is determined using historical returns:

- A beta of 1.0 means that a stock's performance is expected to move exactly like the market or like a broad index, such as the S&P 500. If the S&P 500 is up 10 percent, the stock can be expected to rise 10 percent.

- A beta of 1.5 means that if the S&P 500 is up 10 percent, the stock should rise more than the market, or an increase of 15 percent. If the S&P 500 is down 10 percent, the stock can be expected to decline 15 percent. A higher beta means greater relative volatility. This is a good thing in up markets and a bad thing in down markets.

- A beta of 0.5 means that the stock moves less than the market. If the S&P 500 is up 10 percent, the stock can be expected to rise only 5 percent. A lower beta means lower volatility, which is a good thing in down markets and a bad thing in up markets.

- A beta of 0 means that the performance of the investment is completely unrelated to, or uncorrelated with, the market.

- Beta can be negative, indicating that a stock's performance is expected to move in the opposite direction of the market. If the market rises, the stock will fall. Negative beta is uncommon.

You can also assess the volatility of a portfolio of stocks or a stock mutual fund by looking at the beta for the portfolio or fund. The beta for a portfolio or fund is based on a weighted average beta for all the stocks. With a weighted average, the beta for a holding representing 5 percent of the portfolio will be weighted by 5 percent to determine the weighted average beta for the portfolio. You can find the beta for a stock on most financial websites and beta for a fund on Morningstar.

The return on an investment is a combination of beta and alpha. **Alpha** illustrates how much of the return is not explained by beta. For example, if the beta for a stock is 1.0, the S&P 500 rises 10 percent, and the stock increases 12 percent, the alpha is 2 percent. In other words, the investment performed relatively better than expected given its beta. If the beta of a stock is 1.5, the S&P 500 rises 10 percent, and the investment increases 12 percent, the alpha is –3 percent. In this case, the investment return is positive, but it underperformed relative to expectations.

Valuation Metrics

To determine whether a stock's valuation is attractive, investors consider a number of ratios, or valuation metrics. Investors can compare a stock's valuation metrics to those of other companies in the industry, to the company's peers, or to the overall market using a financial website, such as Yahoo Finance or Morningstar, or a brokerage firm's website.

Price/earnings ratio. A common measure is the **price/earnings ratio**, or the price of a share of stock divided by the stock's earnings per share. **Earnings per share** equals a company's net income divided by the total shares outstanding. **Shares outstanding** are all stock that has been issued by the company that has been sold to investors or is held by insiders. If a company earns $10,000,000 and has 5,000,000 shares outstanding, then earnings per share would be $2.

The price/earnings ratio, also known as the **P/E multiple**, or **P/E**, reflects how much an investor is willing to pay for one share of a company's earnings. For example, if a share of stock is trading at $20 and earnings are $2 per share, the P/E is $20/$2, or 10x. In other words, the investor is willing to pay ten times earnings.

The price/earnings ratio is reported in two ways. Earnings per share can be based on what the company earned in the past twelve months, known as the **trailing twelve months P/E**. Earnings per share may also be based on a consensus estimate of what Wall Street investment analysts expect the company to earn over the next year, known as the **forward P/E**.

Long-term earnings growth. Investors are willing to pay a higher valuation for stocks with stronger earnings growth potential. When investors evaluate a stock as a potential investment, they are looking at what they would pay for one share of what a company is expected to earn this year. In addition, investors are considering what the company is expected to earn next year. In other words, investors are paying not only for this year's earnings but also for future earnings.

When you compare the forward P/E ratio to the long-term earnings growth rate, you determine the **P/E-to-growth ratio**, or the **PEG ratio**. For example, a stock selling at a forward 15 P/E ratio for a company that is expected to achieve long-term earnings growth of 15 percent per year would have a PEG ratio of 1.0. The PEG ratio is helpful because investors can compare the valuations of companies that are growing at different rates.

Price/book value per share. Book value is a company's assets less its liabilities. This is similar to an individual looking at his or her net worth. Book value per share is the total book value of the company divided by the number of shares outstanding. If a company has intangible assets, such as patents, these could also be deducted from book value to determine tangible book value. The **price/book value ratio**, or **price/book ratio**, illustrates how much an investor is willing to pay for one share of the company's book value.

For example, a company has a book value of $50 million and 5 million shares outstanding. Book value per share is $50,000,000/5,000,000, or $10 per share. If a stock selling for $20 has a book value per share of $10, the price/book ratio is $20/$10 or 2x. Another way to say this is that the stock is selling for two times book value. Over time, the value of a company's plant and equipment (which are assets) is reduced by depreciation, or writing down the value of long-lived assets. If a company has a lot of old equipment, the book value is lower because the equipment has been written down over time.

Dividend yield. Dividends are distributions of earnings to equity shareholders. Remember that the dividend yield is the dividend per share divided by the price of a share of stock. If you buy one share of stock for $50 and that share pays a $1 dividend, then the dividend yield is $1 divided by $50, or 2 percent. Companies don't distribute all earnings, because they need to keep capital on hand to fund operations and expansion. The earnings that are not distributed are called **retained earnings** and increase the value of the company. The **dividend payout ratio**

is dividends per share divided by earnings per share. This ratio shows the proportion of earnings that are paid out to shareholders through dividends.

Dividends are an important consideration for a number of reasons. Dividends are a significant component of total return. Remember that total return on an investment is the increase or decrease in the value of the asset plus dividends or income earned while you hold the investment.

Dividends are more than a distribution, however. They are an indication of a company's financial health. A company's ability to pay a dividend signals that the business is doing well. The stocks of companies that increase dividend payouts from time to time tend to perform well over the long run. In order to increase dividends, a management team must be confident in the company's ability to generate profits today and going forward. In contrast, reducing or eliminating a dividend is a very bad sign and will cause the value of a stock to fall significantly. Because of the importance placed on dividends by investors, management teams do not raise dividends unless they are very confident that they can continue to pay them going forward.

Getting Paid to Wait

With dividend-paying stocks, you earn income as you wait for a stock to appreciate. Dividends are an important component of the total return you earn from a stock.

Rather than receiving a cash payment, you can reinvest your dividends back into company stock. Many companies have a **dividend reinvestment plan**, or **DRIP**, through which employees can buy shares directly from the company without having to pay a commission. A DRIP is similar to an automatic savings plan, in that you are building your nest egg and don't really miss the money. At the same time, however, you will have to pay taxes on the dividends. Reinvesting also affects the cost basis, so make sure you keep good records. You can invest through a number of different online brokerage platforms.

TYPES OF STOCKS OR EQUITIES

Domestic stocks are issued by US companies; **international stocks** are issued by international companies. When looking at a multinational company, or a company that does business in many countries, consider where the business actually makes its money. If a company is based in the United States yet most of its sales are generated overseas, it should be considered an international company. Currency fluctuations have an impact on the value of international stocks—in terms of corporate earnings, the value of the stock, and the dividends earned while you are holding the investment.

There are three main types of international stocks based on the characteristics of the geographic region where the issuing company is located: **developed market stocks, emerging market stocks**, and **frontier market stocks**. Examples of countries from the different types of geographic regions are highlighted in figure 6.3.

Developed Markets	Emerging Markets	Frontier Markets
• Canada	• Mexico	• Nigeria
• Switzerland	• China	• Vietnam
• Netherlands	• South Africa	• Morocco
• Japan	• Brazil	• Croatia
• Australia	• Taiwan	• Lebanon

Figure 6.3. Examples of geographic markets.

There are important differences among the three types of geographic regions:

- Stocks from developed economies outside the United States often face many of the same opportunities and risks that domestic stocks do. A major difference, however, is the effect of currency fluctuations. Currency fluctuations have an impact on the value of the stock and dividends received, yet they also have an impact on a foreign company's underlying business. Appreciation in the local currency gives international companies more buying power, but it can also make their goods relatively more expensive for foreigners.

- Emerging market stocks are correlated to US domestic stocks in some ways but not in others. Emerging economies are less stable but grow much faster than developed economies. Because emerging markets look to the United States and developed markets for investment dollars, emerging market stocks are affected by what happens in the United States and in other developed countries. Emerging economies are building infrastructure, so commodity prices are also a consideration, as is geopolitical risk.

- A lesser developed emerging market is referred to as a frontier market. The values of stocks from frontier markets are affected by commodity prices, international funding sources, and geopolitical risk. These economies have greater growth prospects than emerging markets. There is also less economic stability in these regions, however, and some frontier stocks can be quite illiquid.

Other Types of Investable Assets

Some investable assets are more specialized and are used less frequently by retail investors. Even though you are more likely to focus on stocks and bonds when you invest, it is a good idea to be familiar with other asset classes. Remember the financial truth that everything is related. Just like your financial decisions, financial markets are interconnected. Also, your needs and circumstances will change over time. What might not be appropriate today might make sense tomorrow.

Derivatives

Derivatives are a type of investment in which the value is derived from something else. The value of a derivative may depend on changes in the price of a stock, the price of an agricultural product, interest rates, or the exchange rate for a foreign currency. Derivatives are used to reduce risk associated with these fluctuations. Investors can trade derivatives as a way to speculate about the direction of interest rates, exchange rates, or the prices of different types of assets, such as stocks or commodities.

An **option** is a common type of derivative. **Calls** and **puts** provide an investor with the opportunity to buy (call) or sell (put) something in the future at a specific price for a certain period. The specific price is called the **strike price**. An investor pays a premium to acquire the option. With an option, the investor decides whether to buy or sell something—a stock, an agricultural product, or foreign currency—which is called **exercising the option**.

An option is **in the money** if exercising the option results in a profit. For example, a call option is in the money if the price of a stock rises above the option's strike price. In this case, exercising the option makes sense because you will make a profit. If the price of the stock falls below a put option's strike price, the put option is in the money. Exercising the put makes sense because you will make a profit. For an **out of the money** option, exercising the option would result in a loss. If an option is not exercised, it expires worthless, and you lose the premium paid.

Startup companies may offer call options as part of compensation. Compared to larger, more established companies, startups have more limited cash resources. Options are used as an enticement other than salary for employees to stick around for a few years and enjoy the future success of the startup.

Options also can protect the value of your investments by reducing the downside risk. If you work for a company and own company stock, you can use options to reduce the risk of a decline in the stock price. For example, if you buy a put option, you can sell the stock at a fixed price or establish a floor for the value of your company stock.

Futures contracts are another type of derivative. Whereas an option gives you the opportunity to buy or sell something in the future, a futures contract requires you to buy or sell something in the future. Futures contracts are bought or sold by investors, with an exchange acting as a clearinghouse. Futures contracts are common in agriculture, and enable farmers to lock in prices for their crops. You will also see futures used to hedge or reduce the risk associated with currency or interest rate fluctuations.

Counterparty risk is an important consideration for investors. **Counterparty risk** is the risk that another party will default or not honor an agreement. Because options and futures are traded on an exchange, the exchange acts as an intermediary and helps to minimize counterparty risk.

Master Limited Partnerships, or MLPs

Many energy infrastructure and natural resource companies, such as pipeline or timber companies, are structured as **master limited partnerships**, or **MLPs**. Partnerships are taxed differently than traditional companies. Traditional corporations, which are called C corporations for tax purposes, pay taxes on their income. Investors who own stock in the company pay taxes on the portion of income they receive as dividends. Therefore, the corporate income that is distributed as dividends is actually taxed twice: first at the corporate level and second as a dividend.

MLPs involve specific tax and accounting considerations. For MLPs or any partnership, earnings are not taxed at the entity level, and they flow directly through to the partners. The income earned by an MLP is taxed only once. Instead of receiving a 1099 at the end of the year, investors receive a K-1, showing their share of income, gains, and losses.

There is a distinction between the income reported on a K-1 and the distributions received by investors. MLP investors receive distributions, not dividends. Some expenses incurred by natural resource and energy infrastructure companies are noncash. If a pipeline company records depreciation on a piece of equipment, that expense does not represent an actual cash outlay but does reduce net income. Each year, the investor pays taxes on the portion of the distribution that represents net income, as shown on the K-1. The rest of the distribution is tax deferred. It is considered a return of capital and reduces the cost basis. When the investor sells the investment, he or she pays two types of taxes: taxes on the return of capital at ordinary income tax rates, and capital gains taxes if the value of the investment exceeds the cost basis.

Investors may find investing directly in an MLP complicated. MLP funds, however, are structured like a traditional company, or a C corporation. An MLP fund pays taxes at the corporate level, which results in an extra layer of taxation. For an MLP fund, the tax reporting is much simpler, because investors receive a 1099 instead of a K-1.

Although from a tax-reporting perspective, investing in MLP funds is less complicated than directly investing in an MLP, make sure you understand how MLP funds are structured before investing in them. Some MLP funds are closed-end funds that use leverage, or borrow, to enhance returns. I prefer funds that do not use leverage.

Real Estate Investment Trusts, or REITs

Real estate investment trusts, or **REITs**, are funds comprising real estate holdings. A REIT specializes in one type of real estate holding, such as apartment buildings, regional malls, or office buildings. REITs are required to pay out at least 90 percent of taxable net income each year. Distributions are a combination of ordinary income, capital gains, and return of capital, which affects the cost basis. Each year, you pay taxes on the ordinary income and on capital gains. REIT distributions are nonqualified. Like MLPs, REITs can incur noncash expenses, such as depreciation. As a result, the dividends distributed on a REIT could exceed the income earned for a particular year. In those cases, the difference is considered a return of capital. The return of capital reduces your cost basis in the REIT, which will have an impact on the capital gains owed when you sell the investment.

Private Capital

Private capital represents equity investments in private—not publicly traded—companies. Most private capital investments are through funds. Because of high minimum investment requirements, private capital investors are often institutions (pensions, foundations, or endowments) and very high net worth individuals. Private capital funds require a lengthy, multiyear commitment.

There are two main types of private capital funds. **Venture capital funds** invest in early-stage companies—rapidly growing start-up companies that are usually not yet profitable. **Private equity funds** also invest in companies that are growing but are more established or beyond the start-up stage. Private equity investments help companies grow their existing business, and the money may also be used to acquire other businesses to expand the platform.

Alternative Assets

Alternative assets have a unique role in an asset allocation. Compared with stocks and bonds, alternative assets have a low correlation to the financial markets. Having an allocation to alternative assets helps reduce the volatility for your total pool of investable assets. In particular, **hedge funds** aim for a low correlation to stock and bond markets in order to provide protection, or a hedge, for your other investments.

One key feature of hedge funds is that they may **sell short**, or **short**, investments. A hedge fund manager sells short when he or she believes that a stock, bond, or other investment will decline in value. For example, a manager borrows stock and sells it to another investor, and then purchases it later at a (hoped-for) lower price. The ability to buy investments and sell others short can offset some of the downside in the market. Buying some investments, or **being long**, and shorting others is called a **long/short strategy**. A portfolio where some holdings do well when the market rises (the long positions) and others do well when the market falls (the shorts) usually results in lower volatility relative to other asset classes.

In contrast to other types of investments, hedge funds focus on absolute return rather than on relative return. For most investments, performance is evaluated on the basis of **relative return**, or how well an investment performed relative to a market index. In contrast, **absolute return** focuses on a target return, such as 8 percent to 10 percent.

Like private capital funds, the investment minimums for hedge funds are usually very high. Investing in a fund of funds is an easy way to get exposure to a number of different hedge funds and to invest a lower dollar amount. Managers of a fund of funds adjust the allocation to different types of hedge funds and to different hedge fund firms. The fund of funds provides diversified access to the asset class, but there is a cost. In general, hedge fund fees are high compared with other types of investments, and funds of funds add an extra layer on top of the already high fees.

Commodities and Currencies

Investing in commodities, such as metals, energy, and agricultural products, can provide a hedge against inflation. In an inflationary environment, the cost of commodities will rise, and investments in commodities will increase in value. Investing in currencies, such as the British pound, the euro, or the Japanese yen, adds international exposure and diversification to your portfolio. Individual investors often use currencies in specific circumstances, such as to provide a hedge against currency fluctuations for a specific international investment.

CHAPTER 7

Types of Investment Structures: Ways to Invest

JUST AS THERE ARE many types of investable assets, there are many ways to invest. Let's review the most common methods.

| Investable Assets
What to Invest In | Investment Structures
Ways to Invest | Investment Accounts
Why to Invest |
| --- | --- | --- |
| • Cash and money market
• Bonds
• Stocks
• Derivatives
• Master limited partnerships (MLPs)
• Real estate investment trusts (REITs)
• Private capital
• Alternative assets
• Commodities and currencies | • Individual account
• Mutual funds
• Index funds
• Exchange traded funds (ETFs)
• Exchange traded notes (ETNs)
• Target date funds | • Taxable
• 401(k)s and 403(b)s
• Individual retirement accounts (IRAs)
• Roth IRA and 401(k)s
• Annuities
• 529 plans |

Fundamental Investing Concepts

Figure 7.1. Investment structures.

Individual Accounts

People can invest in bonds, stocks, or other securities by working with a professional at a brokerage firm. An individual account with a broker or financial adviser is also known as a **separate account**. You can also manage a separate account by yourself. Many brokerage firms operate online platforms and have physical branches located across the United States. Investors pay a commission for each trade, but firms like these also offer funds without commissions, loads, or transaction fees.

Whether you invest on your own or with a broker, you have the option of using margin in an attempt to increase returns. **Margin accounts** allow investors to borrow against their holdings. The investable assets in the account are collateral for a **margin loan**. The money borrowed with a margin loan enables an investor to put more money to work. Loans, or leverage, can enhance returns, but they also increase risk significantly.

For example, if a stock you own that is used as collateral for a margin loan declines in value, you will face a margin call. With a **margin call**, you will need to put up cash as additional collateral for the margin loan.

Although hedge funds do it, selling stocks short in an individual account is a risky way to enhance returns. Remember that selling a stock short, or shorting a stock, means that you borrow stock and sell it to another investor. You will buy the stock at a later time at what you hope will be a lower price. Selling short can be risky because of the unlimited downside risk. If you buy a stock, the most you can lose is the price paid for it. There is no limit, however, to how high a stock might go. For example, if you sell short stock in a company and another company decides to acquire the company that you are shorting, the stock can rise significantly on the day that the deal is announced. If you have sold short a stock that surges in value quickly, your losses will be large.

Sometimes it is difficult to create a diversified portfolio if you don't have a significant amount of money to invest. In a portfolio, having at least twenty to twenty-five holdings, or **positions**, is preferable. If you do not have enough money to invest in twenty to twenty-five different stocks or bonds, consider an investment fund.

Many different types of funds are discussed in this chapter. Detailed information about funds is available in a fund's prospectus, which can be cumbersome and quite technical. Financial firms are required to provide investors with essential information in the numerous disclosures that accompany marketing materials. The discussion here should help you figure out what information is most important for your investment decisions.

Mutual Funds

Mutual funds offered by asset management firms are the most common type of investment fund. There are different structures and styles of mutual funds. The two main structures are called "open-end" and "closed-end." We will also cover the two main investing approaches for mutual funds—active and passive.

Open-End Mutual Funds

In an **open-end mutual fund**, individuals buy shares directly from the asset management company. The fund's **portfolio manager**, or **PM**, invests money provided by investors who have bought shares in the fund. Asset management firms sell as many shares as investors want to buy. The money going into open-end mutual funds is called an **inflow**. The money coming out of open-end mutual funds is an **outflow**, or **redemption**. The total amount of money in a mutual fund is called **assets under management**, or **AUM**.

Open-end mutual fund shares are priced at the **net asset value**, or **NAV**, at the end of each trading day. Per share NAV is the value of the fund's assets minus its liabilities divided by the number of shares outstanding. If the value of the portfolio holdings rises or falls during the trading day, the NAV rises or falls. Unlike other types of investable assets, you can invest in an open-end mutual fund only at the end of the trading day. Likewise, if you want to sell, or redeem, your shares in an open-end fund, you redeem directly from the fund manager at NAV or sell back your shares to the fund manager at the end of the day.

Although open-end funds can sell an unlimited number of shares to investors, an asset management company might close a fund if the amount of money in the fund grows too large. For a stock fund with substantial AUM, the portfolio manager will need to buy or sell large blocks of stock, which can pose problems. If buy or sell orders are substantial compared to a stock's normal daily trading volume, the large trades can have an impact on the stock's price, or **move the market**.

Portfolio managers are more likely to close small-cap and microcap funds than they are to close large-cap funds because small-cap and microcap companies have fewer shares outstanding. In addition, senior management and employees of a small-cap or microcap company, or **insiders**, might own a large proportion of the stock. Large insider ownership means that there is less stock available to outside investors, or less **float**. Sometimes a mutual fund is closed to new investors, but existing investors can continue to put money in the fund.

Mutual funds carry the risk of **embedded capital gains**. When you invest in a mutual fund, you own a share in a pool of assets. You do not own individual assets or holdings within that pool. This may seem like a subtle distinction, but it is important. On the day that you invest in a mutual fund, your share in the pool of assets could include holdings that have appreciated since the fund manager originally bought them and are valued above cost. You don't get the benefit of that appreciation, however, because you are investing at today's NAV. Other holdings in the pool could be currently valued below the original cost when the portfolio manager first bought them.

For mutual funds, capital gains are realized when the portfolio manager makes a distribution. The manager distributes a certain amount per share in cash to all shareholders of record as of a particular date, thus reducing the level of embedded capital gains in the fund. You will receive documentation from the fund showing the amount of capital gains.

Mutual funds are not as tax efficient as separate, or individually managed, accounts. Table 7.1 uses a hypothetical example to illustrate the difference between investing $1,000 today in a mutual fund and $1,000 today in a separate account.

TABLE 7.1. Risk of embedded capital gains for mutual funds.

Invest $1,000 in a Fund Today
Own 5 Percent of the $20,000 AUM Fund with an Embedded Capital Gain

Fund	Cost Basis	Value	Gain/(Loss)
100 Stock A	$35x100=$3,500	$45x100=$4,500	$1,000
100 Stock B	$30x100=$3,000	$25x100=$2,500	($500)
100 Stock C	$50x100=$5,000	$40x100=$4,000	($1,000)
100 Stock D	$60x100=$6,000	$75x100=$7,500	$1,500
Cash	$1,500	$1,500	$0
Totals	$19,000	$20,000	$1,000

Invest $1,000 in a Separate Account Today
No Embedded Capital Gain

Account	Cost Basis	Value	Gain/(Loss)
5 Stock A	$45x5=$225	$45x5=$225	$0
5 Stock B	$25x5=$125	$25x5=$125	$0
5 Stock C	$40x5=$200	$40x5=$200	$0
5 Stock D	$75x5=$375	$75x5=$375	$0
Cash	$75	$75	$0
Totals	$1,000	$1,000	$0

For the fund, the embedded capital gains are present the day that you invest. Even though you did not benefit from the increased value of the underlying holdings, you are responsible for the capital gains, which could be distributed (and taxable) at any point in time. In a separate account, however, there are no embedded capital gains. You deposit money in the account and begin to make investments. No preexisting holdings have appreciated or have embedded capital gains.

You can analyze the potential for embedded capital gains. Websites such as Morningstar provide an estimate of embedded capital gains for a mutual fund. Morningstar and the fund manager's website will provide a history of distributions from a fund, and you can look up a manager's record of capital gains distributions. Investigate how recently distributions have occurred, as well has how much has been distributed and at what times of year. If a fund appreciates significantly during the year, the likelihood of a capital gains distribution increases. Avoid investing in a mutual fund late in the calendar year because you could be hit with a capital gains distribution and tax bill soon thereafter.

Closed-End Funds

Closed-end funds are not as common as open-end funds. **Closed-end funds** usually comprise income-producing investments, such as bonds or stocks with high dividends. These funds are favored by investors seeking current income. Unlike an open-end fund, which can continue to sell shares to investors, a closed-end fund raises money once, and the number of shares is fixed. There is an initial offering for a closed-end fund just like for a stock or bond. The initial offering involves up-front charges. Some investors wait until after the initial offering to invest in a closed-end fund, so as to avoid paying up-front charges.

Closed-end fund valuations are driven by supply and demand, not daily NAV. Closed-end funds usually trade at a premium or a discount to NAV. If an investor wants to exit a closed-end fund, he or she must sell to another investor. This is unlike open-end funds, where investors redeem directly from the asset management company at NAV or sell back their shares at today's valuation. Open-end funds trade at the end of the day, whereas closed-end funds trade throughout the day.

Actively Managed Mutual Funds

For **actively managed funds**, a portfolio manager researches and chooses the holdings, or securities, that he or she finds the most attractive. The portfolio manager also continues to evaluate existing holdings to see if they should remain in the fund. Actively managed funds invest in stocks, bonds, and other types of securities. When researching potential holdings for a stock fund, for example, the portfolio manager looks at a company's earnings, cash flow, and balance sheet. He or she also looks at factors such as product quality, market share, new product pipelines, and the strength of the management team. In other words, the portfolio manager analyzes a company's fundamental attributes, or its **fundamentals**, along with the stock's valuation, to determine whether to make an investment or to continue to hold the stock in the portfolio. Buying and selling portfolio holdings is called **portfolio turnover**. The level of turnover varies by manager. In addition to increased transaction costs, high portfolio turnover is less tax efficient because of capital gains.

With an actively managed fund, the portfolio manager tries to generate alpha or a return that is better than the index or a comparable benchmark. For equities, active managers are sometimes referred to as "stock pickers." A **stock picker's market** is when the quality of a company's fundamental attributes drives the demand for and performance of stocks. This is also called a "fundamentally driven market." In a stock picker's market, quality is a differentiating factor, and research is instrumental. The same is true for bonds. Doing in-depth research regarding the quality and valuation of a bond is essential for good investment performance in fundamentally driven markets.

In hot markets, or **momentum-driven markets**, there is less emphasis on research and on analyzing an investment's fundamental attributes. In a momentum-driven market, valuations rise across the board. As the saying goes, "A rising tide lifts all boats." Sometimes when the market rises significantly, even lower-quality securities do well. In fact, lower-quality stocks can sometimes appreciate more rapidly than higher-quality securities in a momentum-driven market. For example, when demand for stocks is strong, some lower-quality stocks may appear to be a relative bargain, especially when there is a lot of enthusiasm for a particular sector. Investors may underestimate the risk associated with lower-quality stocks when they see them as more attractively valued opportunities. Lower-quality stocks may be a bargain for a very good reason—volatile earnings, higher debt, lower profit margins, or a weak management team. Remember, value depends on what someone is willing to pay for an asset, not on the quality of the asset. It does not matter if it is a stock picker's market or a momentum-driven market, value is subjective, not objective.

For actively managed stock mutual funds, managers usually have a style or market-cap specialization. With a market-cap specialization, managers invest only in companies of a particular size, such as large-cap or small-cap companies. These size restrictions usually apply only to the initial investment. For example, a small-cap portfolio manager may invest only in companies with a market capitalization of less than $2 billion. If the portfolio manager is a good stock picker, the stocks will appreciate and exceed the $2 billion threshold. Portfolio managers will probably not sell these stocks right away even though the stocks have exceeded the small-cap definition. This is called "letting your winners run."

In addition to market-cap specialization, active managers may focus on a certain investing style. For stock funds, there are two main active management styles. **Growth managers** invest in companies with strong earnings growth. They look at the long-term earnings growth rate, the forward P/E ratio, and the PEG ratio, in addition to the quality of the earnings and the strength of the balance sheet. Growth stock managers tend to invest in stocks with greater than expected earnings growth and, consequently, higher price/earnings multiples. The key is to find stocks that will increase earnings faster than expected. Growth stock portfolios often include companies in fast-growing industries, such as technology, telecommunications, and biotech.

Growth at a Reasonable Price, or GARP

Some growth managers look for companies that are increasing earnings but also have an attractive valuation. Their portfolios are more likely to hold stable growers than high-flying stocks with lofty valuations.

In contrast to growth managers, **value managers** focus primarily on a stock's valuation. Value managers invest in companies that are attractively valued or are trading at a discount to what the portfolio manager thinks the company's underlying assets are worth. Value managers look for lower P/Es, lower price/book ratios, and attractive dividend yields. Utilities pay relatively high dividends and are often included in value portfolios. Value managers tend to prefer stable stocks that can perform well in strong or weak economic environments— these are also known as **defensive stocks**. Utilities and companies that produce consumer staples, such as soap and toothpaste, are examples of defensive stocks.

Some value managers focus on out-of-favor companies and industries or turnaround situations. A company could face a short-term issue, such as a temporary shortage in a raw material that is used in production, or issues related to the weather that have a negative impact on the business. These are examples of short-term factors that should not affect the long-term prospects for a company. Value managers with a long-term orientation are willing to invest in stocks and hold onto them, or to "weather the storm."

In addition to information about performance, risk, and the fundamental attributes for the holdings within an actively managed fund, Morningstar also provides comparisons for index benchmarks and for fund managers with a similar style. You can compare a fund's performance, risk and attributes to a comparable universe such as small-cap value stocks, high-yield bonds, or emerging-markets stocks.

Passive, or Index, Funds

Index funds are a type of mutual fund that replicates the performance of an index. Examples of common indices are:

- S&P 500 for large-cap stocks
- Russell 2000 for small-cap stocks
- MSCI EAFE for international stocks
- Wilshire 5000 for the total stock market
- Barclays US Aggregate for bonds

Because the composition of these funds is based on an index rather than on a portfolio manager choosing stocks or bonds, these funds are called **passive investments**. Compared with actively managed funds, index funds are lower-cost alternatives. Portfolio turnover and transaction costs are lower than for actively managed funds. If an actively managed fund makes a lot of trades, or has high portfolio turnover, transaction costs will be high. When costs are high, managers must charge high fees. In addition, because the composition of an index fund is based on an index, the portfolio manager does not need to research new portfolio ideas. This reduces the expenses associated with managing the fund. For index funds, dividends and interest income from underlying holdings are reinvested into the fund. Distributions are made periodically, usually on a quarterly basis. Index funds are a type of mutual fund, so investors can buy or sell shares only at the end of the day.

Index funds include all the investments in the index, but the amount of each investment varies, depending on how the fund is **weighted**. Most stock index funds are market-cap weighted rather than equal weighted. With a market-cap weighted fund, there is a greater weighting, or emphasis, on the largest-cap companies in the index. A market-cap weighted index will earn higher returns than an equal weighted fund when the largest-cap stocks are performing relatively better than smaller-cap stocks.

At the same time, however, strong performance for large-cap stocks could increase the risk for market-cap weighted funds. If larger-cap stocks are in favor and rise significantly, they will represent an ever-larger proportion of a market-weighted index fund. Therefore, the index fund will have a greater allocation of stocks that have appreciated considerably and could be considered overvalued.

With an equal weighted fund, every stock or bond has the same weight. Compared with a market-cap weighted fund, relatively more emphasis is placed on smaller-cap and midcap holdings. Equal weighted index funds will perform better than market-cap weighted indexes when the stocks of smaller and midsize companies are appreciating more than the shares of larger-cap companies.

A market-cap weighted fund could skew the true exposure to a sector or region. As an illustration, the MSCI Emerging Market

Index is a market-cap weighted index. Because Samsung Electronics is based in South Korea, it is considered an emerging markets stock. Not surprisingly, it is one of the largest holdings in the emerging markets index. Most people think of Samsung as a global brand, however, not as a company from an emerging market.

Fundamental weighted index funds adjust the weighting of the index holdings based on factors such as growth in sales, the dividend yield, and the amount of debt, or leverage, on the company's balance sheet. Relative to a regular market-cap or equal-cap weighted index, fundamental indices can have higher portfolio turnover, which means higher transaction costs and fees.

Exchange Traded Funds, or ETFs

Exchange traded funds, or **ETFs**, are similar to index funds in that they replicate the performance of an index or sector of the economy or the market. There are several distinctions, however. For ETFs, a major brokerage firm, known as an authorized participant, creates a basket of securities. The authorized participant sells shares of the ETF to investors. ETFs trade throughout the day, not just at the end of the day, like a mutual fund. The funds have lower management fees than index funds do. In some cases, you will pay a commission when you invest in an ETF. If you are investing in ETFs regularly through an automatic savings plan, be careful because the commissions can add up. For mutual funds, you pay based on a percentage of assets, not on how many transactions you make. Some brokerage firms offer no-commission ETFs.

Unlike an index fund, ETFs accumulate dividends and interest income from the underlying holdings and make regular distributions rather than reinvesting the income. Compared with mutual funds, ETFs are more tax efficient. Mutual funds distribute capital gains to all shareholders when the portfolio manager decides to make a distribution. An investor realizes a capital gain on an ETF when he or she sells shares or units. Therefore, the investor has control over when capital gains are realized. Sometimes mutual funds can have high minimums for investment; ETFs do not.

Alternative weightings ETFs provide specific exposures to market sectors or strategies. Some focus on a fundamental metric, such as dividend yield or price-to-book value ratio.

Managed ETF portfolios are made up of various ETFs. These portfolios provide access to different types of asset classes and markets, or they can represent a specific investment strategy. Managed ETFs are actively managed, rather than passive, portfolios. Strategists design the portfolios, make allocation decisions across ETFs, and reallocate, or rebalance, from time to time. Managed portfolios are commonly used for online wealth and retirement planning programs, and many financial advisers also use them. Fees are closer to mutual fund fees than to ETF fees because managed ETFs require active management. Because managed ETFs are relatively new, some managers have short track records. Make sure that an ETF's performance track record is compliant with Global Investment Performance Standards, or GIPS, from the CFA Institute. Confirm whether the performance record is actual or hypothetical.

The risks associated with ETFs depend on the structure and composition of the fund. **Physical ETFs** invest in actual underlying assets, and the authorized agent creates a basket of securities. In contrast, **synthetic ETFs** use derivatives to mimic the performance of an index or sector. The use of derivatives for an ETF can be riskier than investing in underlying assets. Synthetic ETFs are more common in Europe than in the United

States because of regulatory and tax differences. Be careful of ETFs that are made up of assets that are not liquid. These assets can become even less liquid in the event of financial turmoil.

Exchange traded notes, or **ETNs**, are a type of unsecured debt security. ETNs do not pay interest like a bond; they generate a return based on the performance of an index. With an ETN, you don't own a stake in a portfolio of assets. The issuer is usually a bank or other financial institution. The principal of the note is neither protected nor guaranteed. There is counterparty risk, so check the creditworthiness of the issuer. ETNs can trade on exchanges, and fees are usually higher for ETNs than for ETFs. Different types of ETNs are taxed differently, so confirm how income on the investment is taxed.

Target date funds change the allocation across various asset classes as retirement approaches. The funds automatically rebalance and change the allocation periodically to meet targets. Allocations are based on how asset classes have performed historically. The automatic rebalancing can be appealing, but investors need to monitor the allocation and performance closely and on a regular basis. Target date fund fees are often fairly high.

Depending on market conditions as your retirement draws near, traditionally safe asset classes may not be as safe. Bonds have appreciated considerably in recent years and may not be as safe an asset class as they were in the past. You should never think of investing as a "set it and forget it" exercise. You may have a different risk tolerance or different needs than other people. If target date funds are appealing, consider using them for only a portion of your asset allocation.

CHAPTER 8

Types of Investment Accounts: Why to Invest

INVESTMENTS RESIDE IN various types of accounts that serve different purposes. Investment accounts may be designed to save for retirement, college, or other general purposes. In this chapter, we will cover taxable accounts, retirement accounts, annuities, and college savings accounts.

Investable Assets *What to Invest In*	Investment Structures *Ways to Invest*	Investment Accounts *Why to Invest*
• Cash and money market • Bonds • Stocks • Derivatives • Master limited partnerships (MLPs) • Real estate investment trusts (REITs) • Private capital • Alternative assets • Commodities and currencies	• Individual account • Mutual funds • Index funds • Exchange traded funds (ETFs) • Exchange traded notes (ETNs) • Target date funds	• Taxable • 401(k)s and 403(b)s • Individual retirement accounts (IRAs) • Roth IRA and 401(k)s • Annuities • 529 plans

Fundamental Investing Concepts

Figure 8.1. Investment accounts.

With investment accounts, it is essential to distinguish whether they are taxable, tax deferred, or tax advantaged. To encourage individuals to save for retirement or a college education, the US government created types of investment accounts that either defer the taxes owed (tax deferred) or grow tax free (tax advantaged). All other types of investment accounts are considered taxable accounts.

Taxable Accounts

Although there are no tax benefits, taxable accounts are more liquid and more flexible than tax-deferred or tax-advantaged accounts. Investors can gain access to funds without penalties like those that exist for the other types of accounts. There are several things to keep in mind or track for taxable accounts.

Dividends and Interest

Interest and nonqualified dividends are taxed at the ordinary income rate, and qualified dividends are taxed at a lower rate. (Remember that the ordinary income rate is the same rate that you pay on your wages or salary.) There are, however, some exceptions:

- For some types of municipal bonds, interest is not subject to federal income taxes or taxes at the state or local level if the bond is issued by the state or municipality where you reside.
- Interest on a municipal bond is taxable if the bond is within a mutual fund.
- Interest on US government bonds is not taxable at the state and local level but is taxable at the federal level.

When deciding among corporate, government, and municipal bonds, you can compute a tax-equivalent yield to compare different options. The **tax-equivalent yield** is the yield on a tax-exempt bond divided by 1 minus your tax rate. This formula allows you to compare two options that are taxed differently:

tax-exempt bond yield ÷ (1 − your tax rate) = tax-equivalent yield

Capital Gains and Losses

Remember that there is a difference in the taxation of short-term capital gains for an investment held one year or less and long-term capital gains for an investment held for more than one year. Short-term capital gains are taxed at the same rate as ordinary income. Long-term capital gains are taxed at rates of up to 20.0 percent. Also remember that you can offset investment gains with losses in a given year. You can also carry forward losses and use them in subsequent years to offset future capital gains. Make sure that you do not buy back a stock within 30 days of selling it, or it will be a wash sale; you cannot realize a loss from a wash sale.

Cost Basis

As you monitor your investments, don't forget to track factors that affect the cost basis and taxation. Both stock splits and reinvested dividends have an impact on cost basis. If you inherit an investment, the cost basis **steps up** in most cases. With inherited securities, the cost basis is not what the person originally paid. Instead the cost basis steps up or is equal to the security's fair market value on the date of death or on an alternative valuation date used for estate tax purposes. When you sell inherited securities, all capital gains are considered long-term and are taxed at the lower rate.

Retirement Accounts

There are many ways to save for retirement. Because fewer and fewer Americans have traditional pension plans, I focus here on other types of retirement accounts—401(k)s, 403(b)s, IRAs, Roth IRAs, and Roth 401(k)s. These accounts all have tax benefits, which are discussed in each section.

401(k) and 403(b) Accounts

A common type of retirement account is a 401(k) plan offered by an employer. With a **401(k) plan**, you invest pretax dollars. Money comes out of your paycheck before it is taxed as income and goes straight into an account. The dollars invested grow tax deferred. When you retire, you pay taxes on withdrawals. This account benefits you because, in retirement, you will no longer be working or you may be working part-time. Your income and your tax bracket may be lower in retirement than during your working years, so you would pay less taxes than when you are working full-time.

Some companies offer to match 401(k) contributions up to a specific amount. A corporate match is free money, and it is essential that you take full advantage of these opportunities. Not only is the match free, but saving this way will help you ramp up your retirement savings.

MYFL Golden Rule 7
Always take advantage of retirement plan matches.
In the long run, you will be very glad that you did.

A **403(b) plan** is like a 401(k) plan, but it is for employees of the government and nonprofit organizations. In the past, 403(b) accounts could invest only in annuities. Now these plans have more investment options. Annuities can have high fees, which has a negative impact on the growth of your savings.

Traditional IRAs

Individual retirement accounts, or **IRAs**, are funded with pretax dollars. These accounts grow tax deferred, as a 401(k) does, and you pay taxes when you withdraw the money upon retirement. But there are restrictions on contributions, depending on your age, income level, and whether you are eligible for a retirement plan at work. Currently, individuals are allowed to put away $5,500 in an IRA each year (or $6,500 if they are age fifty or older.) A **simplified employee pension plan**, or **SEP plan**, is an option for self-employed people or those who work at small firms. These are also called **SEP IRAs**.

When you leave a job or retire, you can roll over your 401(k) or 403(b) into an IRA. You will probably have a variety of jobs during your lifetime. By rolling over your 401(k) or 403(b) into an IRA, you will put all your money in one pool, making it much easier to analyze your retirement savings. Remember that it is important to take a comprehensive view of your financial life. Consolidating your retirement accounts into one pool is easier to monitor.

Roth IRAs and Roth 401(k)s

In contrast to traditional IRAs and 401(k)s, **Roth IRAs** and **Roth 401(k)s** are funded with after-tax dollars. The contributions do not reduce your taxable income. In other words, you make contributions to a Roth from your take-home pay after it has been taxed. Roth retirement accounts grow tax free. Moreover, you do not pay taxes on withdrawals if the account has been open for at least five years. A Roth is an example of a tax-advantaged account. Some employers offer Roth 401(k) plans. Contributions to Roth IRAs are limited to those who earn below a threshold amount, whereas contributions to Roth 401(k)s are not. Currently, the IRS limits Roth IRA contributions to those making less than $135,000 or $199,000 if married.

When you are just starting out, it is important to max out your 401(k) or 403(b) contributions and take advantage of any corporate matches as soon as possible. A Roth IRA is a great way to augment your retirement savings, especially when you are young. Once you contribute to a Roth IRA with after-tax dollars, you never pay taxes again. The longer you have until retirement, the greater your benefit from the tax-advantaged status of Roth IRAs.

. . . .

My friend had a wonderful gift idea for her son's college graduation. She helped him set up a Roth IRA and made a contribution. Think about how her gift—and future contributions—will grow until he retires. Moreover, the gift will never be taxed. It is truly a gift that keeps on giving,

. . . .

It is possible to convert a 401(k), 403(b), or IRA into a Roth IRA. With a Roth conversion, you pay taxes when converting the account. There are several things to consider if you are thinking of converting to a Roth IRA. It is a good option for those who think that their marginal tax rate will be higher when they retire. The further away you are from retirement, the greater the advantage of a Roth IRA. Don't convert to a Roth IRA if you need to borrow money from the account to pay the taxes due upon conversion. If you convert to a Roth IRA following a period of significant market appreciation, you will pay a larger tax bill than if you convert when asset values are depressed.

Withdrawing from a Retirement Account

You can begin withdrawing from retirement accounts at age 59½. If you withdraw money from a retirement account before age 59½, you will pay a 10 percent penalty to the IRS in addition to any regular income taxes owed. Certain situations where the penalty does not apply are listed on the IRS's website.

Required minimum distributions, or **RMDs**, are the required minimum amounts that you must withdraw from an IRA each year, beginning at age 70½. RMD tables are available on the IRS's website and are based on life expectancy. For those just starting out in the workforce, RMDs are not top of mind. If you inherit an IRA from someone who started taking withdrawals, however, you will be required to take withdrawals regardless of your age, although the RMD is based on your life expectancy, not on that of the person who passed away. There are no RMDs for a Roth IRA unless the Roth IRA is inherited. For inherited Roth IRAs, consult the IRS website, because the rules can be complex.

Annuities

Annuities are contracts offered by insurance companies and are often used to save for retirement. Annuities provide contract holders a future payment or series of payments, which can be fixed or variable. The growth in the annuity is tax deferred. When you receive the money, you pay taxes on the earnings at ordinary income rates.

There are two main types of annuities. With a **fixed annuity**, you receive a predetermined return. The return can be a specific amount, or it can be tied to a market index. Fixed annuities are not securities but rather are an insurance product and are regulated by state insurance departments.

With a **variable annuity**, you choose among investment options and you bear the investment risk. Variable annuities are considered securities and are regulated by the Securities and Exchange Commission (SEC).

Annuities are complex and can be expensive: you may pay an up-front commission to a salesperson and pay administrative fees. There are underlying expenses for the fund options offered through a variable annuity. In addition, you will likely pay a surrender fee to the annuity provider if you withdraw early in the contract. There can be other fees for added benefits, such as a guaranteed minimum return or for mortality risk. If you withdraw money before the age of 59½, you will pay taxes on the income earned plus a 10 percent penalty to the IRS. There are some exceptions, which you can find on the IRS website. Annuities are a contract but not a guarantee. Contracts can be broken, so annuities carry counterparty risk.

For most people, it does not make sense to invest in an annuity within an IRA account, because an annuity already grows tax deferred. Originally, 403(b) plans were required to use annuities. Now 403(b) plans also offer mutual fund options, which usually have much lower fees than annuities. Compared with other options, the various fees associated with annuities can add up.

529 Plans

The most common type of college savings programs is a **529 plan**. Assets in a 529 plan grow tax-free. Contributions to the plan are not tax deductible at the federal level, but they may be at the state level. Withdrawals are tax-free at the federal level as long as the money is used for qualifying expenses. Depending on the state, there can be additional tax benefits for withdrawals.

With a 529, be careful about the timing of tuition and other related payments and the timing of account withdrawals. In addition, confirm which expenses are qualified and which are not. Qualified expenses are primarily tuition, room, board, books, and mandatory fees, or equipment required for coursework. Recent tax law changes mean that 529 plans also can be used for K–12 private school tuition. There are penalties for early withdrawals and for withdrawals for uses other than qualified expenses. For withdrawals for nonqualified expenses, you will pay taxes on the portion that represents income, or investment earnings. Remember that 529 accounts are funded with after-tax dollars.

529 Plans: Start Early

If you're just starting a family, setting up a 529 plan as early as possible has many benefits. The earlier you start, the longer the money will grow tax-free. Plus, funding a 529 plan can be a "family affair," with grandparents, aunts, and uncles contributing toward a child's education.

Putting Everything to Work

The four chapters in this section have covered a lot of information about investing. Now that you have gotten organized, have taken an objective look at your finances, and are familiar with some investing concepts, it is time to put your knowledge into practice. You are ready to be more actively involved in managing your financial life.

PART 4

Save and Invest Your Money

Many receive advice; only the wise profit from it.

—HARPER LEE

Now that you are familiar with some fundamental investing concepts and various types of assets, investments, and accounts, it is time to save and invest. Begin with determining your goals. When you are just starting out, you may have a number of goals—and a number of financial obligations. This section covers topics such as articulating your savings goals, choosing among different investment choices and platforms, monitoring your investments, and developing a plan to move forward.

....

CHAPTER 9

Determine Your Savings Goals: What Are You Saving For?

*B*EFORE YOU INVEST, it is essential that you think about your savings goals. To do this, you need to articulate your needs and what you expect from your money. To determine your needs, ask yourself the following questions:

- What are your long-term plans—having children, a change in work status, travel, starting a business, purchasing a condo or home?
- Are there any impending near-term changes in your life?
- Do you have plans to go back to school?
- Are there special factors to consider, such as health issues?

Answering these questions will help you evaluate your priorities and needs. Once you have a handle on these, you can start to set savings goals that will help guide your plan. Whatever you are saving for—graduate school, retirement, a home—setting concrete savings goals and articulating them increases the likelihood that you will achieve what you want.

Imminent Need: Emergency Fund

The most immediate savings goal is an emergency fund. Experts recommend that you have an emergency fund sufficient to cover living expenses for at least six months. Emergency funds are vital in case you lose your job or have major repairs to your home or car. Make sure that the assets in your emergency fund are very liquid, such as cash in a savings account or in a money market fund.

You may actually need an emergency fund that is bigger than six months of living expenses. You could face hurdles when looking for a new job, such as geographic restrictions or the need for flexibility in terms of travel or work hours.

Let's revisit the asset allocation grid (table 9.1), which shows the total for each type of asset class across various financial accounts. Remember that your asset allocation grid is like a dashboard for your financial life. The total in the cash and money market fund category represents the emergency fund. Your emergency fund doesn't necessarily have to be all in one account. Using the asset allocation grid, you can track the total amount in cash and money market across all your investments. Remember that your emergency fund cannot come from tax-advantaged or tax-deferred accounts like 529 plans, 401(k)s, or IRAs. If you work with a financial adviser, make sure to let him or her know if you are counting on the money market funds in the taxable account they manage as part of your emergency fund.

If you need to dip into your emergency fund, replenish it as soon as possible. Of course, you hope you won't need to dip into it again soon, but you never know. Replenishing your emergency fund must be a top priority. Better safe than sorry.

Long-Term Need: Retirement Savings

After you have established an emergency fund, retirement should be your next priority. As you plan for retirement, remember that

TABLE 9.1. Emergency fund assets as of January X, XXXX.

	Cash/ money market	Corporate bonds	Domestic stocks	Int'l stocks	Total account	% of total assets
Checking account	$2,000				**$2,000**	4%
Taxable investments						
Brokerage account	$1,000		$3,000		**$4,000**	9%
Mutual funds	$13,000				**$13,000**	29%
Retirement						
401(k)		$2,000	$7,000	$3,000	**$12,000**	27%
IRA		$3,000	$9,000	$2,000	**$14,000**	31%
Total investable assets	**$16,000**	**$5,000**	**$19,000**	**$5,000**	**$45,000**	100%
% of total assets	**36%**	**11%**	**42%**	**11%**	**100%**	
By type:						
Taxable	$19,000	42%				
Retirement	$26,000	58%				
Total investable assets	**$45,000**	**100%**				

we are living longer than our parents were expected to. According to the Social Security Administration, a baby born in 1953 has a life expectancy at birth of sixty-six years if male and seventy-two years if female. A baby born in 1988 has a life expectancy of seventy-one years if male and seventy-eight years if female.[6]

Living longer also means we should plan for a longer retirement. The Social Security Administration projects that more than one in three sixty-five-year-olds will live to age ninety.[7]

Saving enough for retirement should be one of your biggest concerns and is one of the most important topics addressed in this book. When you are just starting out, retirement seems a long way off. There are so many unknowns—where you will live, how much money you will need for day-to-day expenses, whether you will work part time, the state of your health, how long you will live. Many people find the retirement planning process daunting. But it is important to start thinking about the unknowns and variables now, even though retirement may be decades away. Do not postpone thinking about and planning for it. Those who postpone thinking about retirement are already behind.

You will likely need multiple sources of savings to fund your retirement:

- Most Americans working today do not have a defined benefit pension plan or a traditional pension (figure 9.1). The primary sources of retirement funds come from defined contribution pension plans, such as 401(k)s and 403(b)s, and from IRAs.
- Social Security is a source of retirement funds. You can go to ssa.gov/estimator to estimate your future Social Security benefits based on the amount of money you've put into Social Security so far.
- Even with retirement plans and Social Security, you need to plan to supplement to your retirement resources with personal savings.

Although your eligibility for Social Security is decades in the future, you need to understand how it works. The timing of when you start taking Social Security benefits is important,

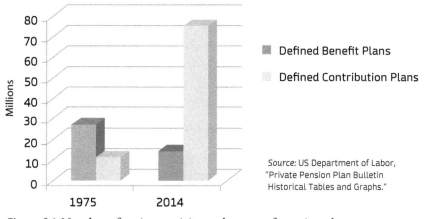

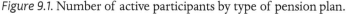

Figure 9.1. Number of active participants by type of pension plan.

because the timing has a big impact on the amount of money you will receive and on your retirement planning.

Social Security is an insurance program. Insurers use actuaries to project outcomes such as longevity. The amount of your monthly Social Security benefit is based on your lifetime average earnings and your life expectancy. Social Security benefits are based on a type of life expectancy table that tends to understate actual life expectancies. This is a good thing, because you will likely live longer than the Social Security Administration thinks you will. The financial incentive to delay collecting benefits is also based on data that assumes shorter life expectancy. If you can afford to, it is advantageous to delay taking Social Security.

Let's walk through the math. For those born after 1960, if you take benefits at the first opportunity—age sixty-two—rather than waiting until the full retirement age of sixty-seven, the amount you receive each month could decrease by 30 percent. Taking benefits at sixty-two will also reduce the amount your spouse receives as a survivor. If you work past full retirement and delay taking Social Security until seventy, the annual increase in benefits will be 8 percent. In the investing world, a guaranteed 8 percent return is very attractive. As an illustration, that is a better annual return than you would have earned investing in the S&P 500 over the past twenty years.

Retirement Planning Calculators

Even with Social Security and an employer-sponsored plan, you should anticipate supplementing your retirement nest egg with personal savings. Retirement planning tools and guidelines can provide an estimate of what you need to save. Many financial websites offer retirement calculators. Compare a few calculators—you may get different answers. With longer-term savings goals, it is difficult to predict your future salary or how much items will cost in the future. Nonetheless, trying different scenarios will help you understand the numbers and gauge your progress toward your retirement savings goals.

The outputs, or answers, derived from retirement calculators are only as good as the inputs. When trying different scenarios, some experts suggest that you assume that you will need 70 to 85 percent of your preretirement salary after you retire. But it is challenging to estimate your salary in twenty, thirty, or forty years, so try different scenarios. Working through the numbers may not give you precise answers, but the exercise illustrates the importance of building a nest egg.

Retirement Planning Guidelines

I like to base my retirement savings goal on a common guideline, which is to build a retirement fund that is equal to a multiple of preretirement income. Experts suggest striving for a multiple from eight to fifteen times your salary at age sixty-five. Like working with a retirement calculator, predicting your salary in the future can be difficult. Try different scenarios—earning $50,000, $70,000, and $90,000—to see the different amounts you would need to accumulate by age sixty-five. If you plan to retire before age sixty-five, or if you have a high income and a high standard of living, aim for the upper end of the range.

As you think about your retirement savings, it is essential to start planning early and chart your progress over time. The previous methods ask you to make assumptions about your salary at retirement. I think comparing your level of retirement savings to your current salary, or your current multiple, helps you determine whether or not you are on track. You can look at your retirement savings divided by your current salary and think about how many years until you plan to retire. If you are halfway to retirement, are you halfway to your desired multiple?

There are a number of advantages to computing your multiple based on your current salary. First, you don't have to estimate your future income. No matter what your age is, you can compare your retirement savings balance with your current salary to assess your progress. Computing the multiple based on your current salary will help you determine whether you need to ramp up savings. For example, if you are thirty-five and make $60,000 per year and your retirement savings are $120,000, then your multiple is 2x. If you are thinking about retiring early, you will need to ramp up your savings. Also, many people don't start thinking about whether or not they have saved enough for retirement savings until they are in their forties or older. Not surprisingly, those who put off thinking about whether or not they are saving enough for retirement are likely behind. Based on these savings factors, you need to start saving before you turn thirty. In the next chapter, we move on to how to achieve retirement and other long-term savings goals that you have set.

Intermediate-Term Needs: Down Payment, School, Other Goals

Your intermediate savings goals depend on lifestyle choices. Although these savings goals are important, they should come after you have established an emergency fund and are making regular contributions toward your retirement savings. Having an adequate emergency fund and being on track for retirement take precedence over intermediate goals.

For intermediate-term needs, I recommend that you focus on one need or goal at a time. To get to that intermediate-term goal, some investors save a **fixed percentage** of their income, such as 5 percent, depending on their goal. This strategy is appealing because it is simple to follow. A fixed percentage gives you the flexibility to save more if your income goes up and save less in a down year. This flexibility makes it easier to stick to your savings plan.

Another way to establish a savings goal is to set a dollar amount for savings and a timeline. You savings goal could be, "I want to save between $x and $y over the next three years." This is a good plan if you are saving for something specific, such as a down payment or graduate school. You can arrange to have a fixed dollar amount transferred from your checking account into savings every pay period. This is called "paying yourself first." Whatever method you use to meet your intermediate goals, the important advice here is to develop a plan.

Time Is Your Friend

When you are just starting out, time can play a big role in how you manage your financial life. In terms of savings and investing, time is your friend in two ways. First, different goals have different time horizons. Some are imminent—such as establishing an emergency fund—and some, like retirement, are longer term in nature. Trying to tackle all your savings goals at once is overwhelming and unrealistic. Thinking about time horizons will help you prioritize your goals and adopt a more methodical and organized approach to working toward them. Figure 9.2 shows an example of different goals, different time horizons, and how to prioritize various financial needs. The goals and plans listed in figure 9.2 are for illustrative purposes only. Remember: Everyone's financial needs and goals are unique.

I cannot overemphasize the positive impact that time has on growing your money. Starting early and contributing regularly to retirement and savings plans have a dramatic effect on how much money you will accumulate over time. Table 9.2 shows the effect of saving different amounts over time. Saving $1,000 or $2,000 per year makes a big difference in the size of your nest egg after thirty years. If you save more than that, the impact is even greater.

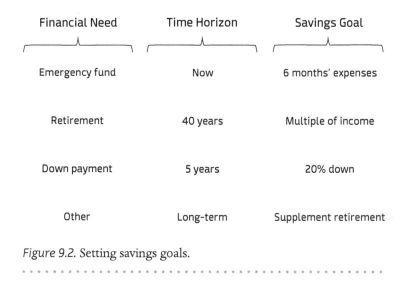

Financial Need	Time Horizon	Savings Goal
Emergency fund	Now	6 months' expenses
Retirement	40 years	Multiple of income
Down payment	5 years	20% down
Other	Long-term	Supplement retirement

Figure 9.2. Setting savings goals.

TABLE 9.2. Impact of regular savings.

Assumed return	7.0 percent

Assumed fee	1.0 percent

Year	Initial	Year-end balance	Initial and additions	Year-end balance	Initial and additions	Year-end balance
1	$1,000	$1,060	$1,000	$1,060	$2,000	$2,120
2	$0	$1,124	$1,000	$2,184	$2,000	$4,367
3	$0	$1,191	$1,000	$3,375	$2,000	$6,749
4	$0	$1,262	$1,000	$4,637	$2,000	$9,274
5	$0	$1,338	$1,000	$5,975	$2,000	$11,951
6	$0	$1,419	$1,000	$7,394	$2,000	$14,788
7	$0	$1,504	$1,000	$8,897	$2,000	$17,795
8	$0	$1,594	$1,000	$10,491	$2,000	$20,983
9	$0	$1,689	$1,000	$12,181	$2,000	$24,362
10	$0	$1,791	$1,000	$13,972	$2,000	$27,943
11	$0	$1,898	$1,000	$15,870	$2,000	$31,740
12	$0	$2,012	$1,000	$17,882	$2,000	$35,764
13	$0	$2,133	$1,000	$20,015	$2,000	$40,030
14	$0	$2,261	$1,000	$22,276	$2,000	$44,552
15	$0	$2,397	$1,000	$24,673	$2,000	$49,345
16	$0	$2,540	$1,000	$27,213	$2,000	$54,426
17	$0	$2,693	$1,000	$29,906	$2,000	$59,811
18	$0	$2,854	$1,000	$32,760	$2,000	$65,520
19	$0	$3,026	$1,000	$35,786	$2,000	$71,571
20	$0	$3,207	$1,000	$38,993	$2,000	$77,985
21	$0	$3,400	$1,000	$42,392	$2,000	$84,785
22	$0	$3,604	$1,000	$45,996	$2,000	$91,992
23	$0	$3,820	$1,000	$49,816	$2,000	$99,631
24	$0	$4,049	$1,000	$53,865	$2,000	$107,729
25	$0	$4,292	$1,000	$58,156	$2,000	$116,313
26	$0	$4,549	$1,000	$62,706	$2,000	$125,412
27	$0	$4,822	$1,000	$67,528	$2,000	$135,056
28	$0	$5,112	$1,000	$72,640	$2,000	$145,280
29	$0	$5,418	$1,000	$78,058	$2,000	$156,116
30	$0	$5,743	$1,000	$83,802	$2,000	$167,603
		Difference		$78,059		$161,860

Note: Assumes that the initial investment and any additions are made at the beginning of the year.

How to Save for Multiple Goals

As you save for multiple goals—emergency fund, retirement, down payment—you also have to consider paying down debt. Managing student loan debt is a reality for most recent college grads, and it can hinder your ability to save. As covered in Part 2, address credit card debt immediately. Paying off credit card debt ranks with establishing an emergency fund in terms of financial priorities.

How do you work toward multiple financial goals at the same time? To manage several savings goal and financial obligations, let's revisit your personal income statement and the 50/20/30 rule. As a reminder, under the 50/20/30 rule, you categorize your expenses as a percentage of your take-home pay. Start with your take-home pay:

- 50 percent goes toward essentials
- 20 percent goes toward savings and debts
- 30 percent is available for everything else

Let's say you start with take-home pay of $45,000 but you have car loan payments and student loan payments. The aggregate of your debt payments and savings is $9,180, or 20 percent of your take home pay. At the end of the year, you are able to save $3,300 or 7 percent of your take home pay.

MYFL Golden Rule 8

Saving and managing your debts should both be priorities. Like boosting your savings, paying down debt has a positive effect on your net worth.

The 50/20/30 rule is a recommendation; you may need to revise the ratios if you have substantial student-loan or other debt payments and want to increase your savings further. Begin with a detailed analysis of the "everything else," or the

TABLE 9.3. Multiple savings goals at current spending levels.

Income

| Take-home pay after taxes | $45,000 | | | | | |

Expenses	*Monthly*	*Annual*	*% of Take-home Pay*	*Essentials*	*Savings and debts*	*Other*
Fixed						
Rent (includes utilities)	$925	$11,100	25%	25%		
Insurance (renters, auto)	$180	$2,160	5%	5%		
Car payment	$220	$2,640	6%		6%	
Parking	$150	$1,800	4%	4%		
Cell phone	$80	$960	2%	2%		
Cable	$65	$780	2%			2%
Health club	$80	$960	2%			2%
Student loan payment	$270	$3,240	7%		7%	
		$23,640	53%			
Variable						
Food and gas	$540	$6,480	14%	14%		
Clothing, home items, etc.	$330	$3,960	9%			9%
Leisure and all other	$635	$7,620	17%			17%
		$18,060	40%			
Total expenses		$41,700	93%			
Net income		**$3,300**	**7%**		**7%**	
				$22,500	$9,180	$13,320
			Totals	**50%**	**20%**	**30%**

30 percent category. You can look cut back on your "everything else" expenditures to ramp up your savings.

Table 9.4 is an example of reallocating to ramp up your savings. If you are able to reduce the spending under "clothing, home items, etc." by $100 a month and "leisure and all other" by $245 a month, then you can put $345 a month directly into savings. Increasing your annual savings by $4,140 a year brings your total percentage of savings from 20 percent of take-home pay to 30 percent. Little changes every month can have a big impact. Depending on your situation, it might make sense to budget 30 percent for debt payments and savings rather than 20 percent.

Unless you are facing an absolute emergency, do not borrow from your retirement account. You may be tempted to borrow from retirement to start a business, to pay for grad school, or to help your children with college tuition down the road. If you borrow from your retirement, you will miss the growth opportunity for the money that you borrowed. Paying yourself back could take longer than expected. Borrowing from your retirement account also means that the planning calculations that you made previously are no longer valid.

One More Goal: Investing in Others

When it comes to managing your financial life, also consider philanthropy, or investing in others. *Webster's* defines philanthropy as "an act or gift done or made for humanitarian purposes." As you develop your spending and savings goals, consider the causes you wish to support.

Take a Hands-on Approach

Increasingly, individuals are taking a more hands-on, engaged approach to philanthropy than in the past. Some refer to it as "venture philanthropy," due to the similarity to venture capital.

TABLE 9.4. Multiple savings goals at reduced spending levels.

Income						
Take-home pay after taxes	$45,000					

Expenses	Monthly	Annual	% of Take-home Pay	Essentials	Savings and debts	Other
Fixed						
Rent (includes utilities)	$925	$11,100	25%	25%		
Insurance (renters, auto)	$180	$2,160	5%	5%		
Car payment	$220	$2,640	6%		6%	
Parking	$150	$1,800	4%	4%		
Cell phone	$80	$960	2%	2%		
Cable	$65	$780	2%			2%
Health club	$80	$960	2%			2%
Student loan payment	$270	$3,240	7%		7%	
		$23,640	53%			
Variable						
Food and gas	$540	$6,480	14%	14%		
Clothing, home items, etc.	**$230**	**$2,760**	**6%**			**6%**
Leisure and all other	**$390**	**$4,680**	**11%**			**10%**
		$13,920	31%			
Total expenses		$37,560	83%			
Net income		**$7,440**	**17%**		**17%**	
				$22,500	**$13,320**	**$9,180**
			Totals	**50%**	**30%**	**20%**

Venture philanthropy represents a deliberate and thoughtful approach to giving. Venture philanthropists regard donations as investments. Rather than support general funding for a large charitable organization, venture philanthropists are likely to become engaged in a specific fundraising initiative that is meaningful to them.

Evaluate donations the same way that you analyze investments. Ask yourself where your donations will have the biggest impact. To ensure that your donation dollars will do the most good possible, look for organizations that use resources efficiently and effectively. Analyze the percentage of donations to an organization that are used to cover administrative and fundraising expenses. If you donate to organizations that spend a low percentage of donations on these expenses, your donations will go further and can have a greater impact. The percentage of donations spent on administration and fundraising should be available in a charity's literature. Visit Charity Navigator at www.charitynavigator.org to look up a charity.

Share Your Time and Talents

Many millennials lack the financial resources to support charities. In truth, there are many facets to philanthropy besides contributing financially. We have numerous opportunities to support important causes—and not all involve money. You can help worthy causes by donating your time and your talents. Most organizations are happy for you to share your time and, especially, your talents and skills. Not only can you offer a needed service but helping a nonprofit as a volunteer may be an opportunity to add something to your resume.

CHAPTER 10

Achieving Your Savings Goals: How Will You Get There?

IN THE PREVIOUS CHAPTER, we focused on setting goals and determining the amount you need to achieve them. This chapter expands on the topic of retirement planning, so you can figure out the steps you need to take to get you to your goals. For those just starting out in the work force—actually, for all of us—you must be consistent, disciplined, and realistic when it comes to saving for retirement.

- It is important to start when you are young and to be consistent about saving and investing each year.
- You must be disciplined and not touch the money once you invest it.
- As you plan, it is essential that you assume a reasonable rate of return for your investments.

By now you have heard about the importance of starting early and the detrimental impact of dipping into your retirement nest egg. But the third point above is not discussed frequently, so let's start with assumptions for returns—or what you can expect to earn on your investments.

Assumptions for Investment Returns and Growing Your Savings

As you think about how much money you need to save and invest each year to meet your goals, consider the expected returns for your investment portfolio over the long run. Given volatility in the markets, setting a fixed investment return goal for each year is unrealistic; trying to achieve a certain average return or range of returns over a period of years is more realistic.

No one can predict how investments, or the financial markets, will perform in a given year or over a long-term horizon. But even though planning for the future involves uncertainty, you need to make some assumptions about growth in your investments to gauge your progress toward attaining your goals.

Simple Calculations to Estimate Growth

To give you a sense of how quickly your money can grow, some helpful rules illustrate the power of compounding investment returns. Remember the fundamental concept of compound growth. When you invest, you earn a return on the dollars that you have contributed. You also earn a return on the growth in your investments.

- **The Rule of 72** calculates how long it takes an investor to double his or her money. As an illustration, assuming an investment generates a return of 7 percent, the number of years to double your investment is 72/7, or a little over ten years.
- According to the **Rule of 7s**, it takes ten years to double your money if you earn 7 percent. An investment with a higher return, such as 10 percent, would take only seven years to double your money.

If you invest $100 and earn 7 percent, you will have $200 after 10 years without making any additional contributions to the account. Compounded growth is your money working for you, and it has a powerful impact, especially over the long run.

What Annual Return Should You Use to Plan?

The Rule of 72 and the Rule of 7s have both been around a long time. Historically, a 7 percent return has been a reasonable assumption for growth. Some industry professionals have commented that individuals can assume long-term investment returns of 7 percent, 8 percent, and even as high as 10 percent if they take on more risk. Some retirement calculators incorporate a 7 percent or 8 percent rate of return. What rate of return should you use for planning?

It is true that the **compounded annual growth rate**, or **CAGR**, for the S&P 500 since 1970 is approximately 11 percent. A blended portfolio of 60 percent allocated to the S&P 500 and 40 percent allocated to the Barclays US Aggregate Bond Index would have generated a compounded annual return of approximately 10 percent since 1976, which is the first year that the Barclays Index was available.

The compounded annual returns for the markets have come down over the past four decades, as illustrated by table 10.1. I believe this trend is due in part to increased correlation across markets. In addition, interest rates in recent years have been at artificially low levels due to central bank policies. Although financial market returns have come down, the standard deviation, or volatility, within the market is still fairly high. In more recent periods—the past ten or twenty years—compounded annual returns have been in the 7 percent range or lower, depending on the time frame and mix within a portfolio.

For planning, I prefer to use an average annual return of 6 percent after fees. If you assume a rate of return on your investments that is too optimistic, you will likely fall short of your goals.

TABLE 10.1. Long-term returns for equity and bond benchmarks

Year	S&P 500 Total Return	Barclays US Aggregate Bond Index	Balanced: 60% Equity/40% Bond
1976	23.8%	15.6%	20.5%
1977	-7.2%	3.0%	-3.1%
1978	6.6%	1.4%	4.5%
1979	18.4%	1.9%	11.8%
1980	32.5%	2.7%	20.6%
1981	-4.9%	6.3%	-0.4%
1982	21.6%	32.6%	26.0%
1983	22.6%	8.4%	16.9%
1984	6.3%	15.2%	9.8%
1985	31.7%	22.1%	27.9%
1986	18.7%	15.3%	17.3%
1987	5.3%	2.8%	4.3%
1988	16.6%	7.9%	13.1%
1989	31.7%	14.5%	24.8%
1990	-3.1%	9.0%	1.7%
1991	30.5%	16.0%	24.7%
1992	7.6%	7.4%	7.5%
1993	10.1%	9.8%	9.9%
1994	1.3%	-2.9%	-0.4%
1995	37.6%	18.5%	29.9%
1996	23.0%	3.6%	15.2%
1997	33.4%	9.7%	23.9%
1998	28.6%	8.7%	20.6%
1999	21.0%	-0.8%	12.3%
2000	-9.1%	11.6%	-0.8%
2001	-11.9%	8.4%	-3.8%
2002	-22.1%	10.3%	-9.2%
2003	28.7%	4.1%	18.8%
2004	10.9%	4.3%	8.3%
2005	4.9%	2.4%	3.9%
2006	15.8%	4.3%	11.2%
2007	5.5%	7.0%	6.1%
2008	-37.0%	5.2%	-20.1%
2009	26.5%	5.9%	18.2%
2010	15.1%	6.5%	11.7%
2011	2.1%	7.8%	4.4%
2012	16.0%	4.2%	11.3%
2013	32.4%	-2.0%	18.6%
2014	13.7%	6.0%	10.6%
2015	1.4%	0.6%	1.0%
2016	12.0%	2.7%	8.2%
2017	21.8%	3.5%	14.5%

(continued)

TABLE 10.1. Long-term returns for equity and bond benchmarks *(continued)*.			
1976–2017	S&P 500 Total Return	Barclays US Aggregate Bond Index	Balanced: 60% Equity/40% Bond
High	37.6%	32.6%	29.9%
Low	-37.0%	-2.9%	-20.1%
CAGR	11.6%	7.5%	10.3%
Median	15.4%	6.4%	11.2%
Std. Dev.	16.1%	6.8%	10.6%
1998–2017	S&P 500 Total Return	Barclays US Aggregate Bond Index	Balanced: 60% Equity/40% Bond
High	32.4%	11.6%	20.6%
Low	-37.0%	-2.0%	-20.1%
CAGR	7.2%	5.0%	6.8%
Median	12.8%	4.8%	9.4%
Std. Dev.	17.9%	3.6%	10.2%
2008–2017	S&P 500 Total Return	Barclays US Aggregate Bond Index	Balanced: 60% Equity/40% Bond
High	32.4%	7.8%	18.6%
Low	-37.0%	-2.0%	-20.1%
CAGR	8.5%	4.0%	7.3%
Median	14.4%	4.7%	10.9%
Std. Dev.	19.3%	3.0%	11.3%

How much do you need to save each year? Let's walk through the math, using an assumption of 6 percent average annual return after fees. Say you are a millennial and you want to save $1 million by the time you retire. Millennials are those born between 1981 and 1997.

The youngest millennials will be in the workforce for forty-five years or more. To save $1 million over forty-five years, one would need to save and invest $4,500 a year (figure 10.1).

As an alternative, you could ramp up over time. Start with $2,000, $3,000, 4,000, then $4,800 for the remainder of the time horizon, and you will still reach your goal.

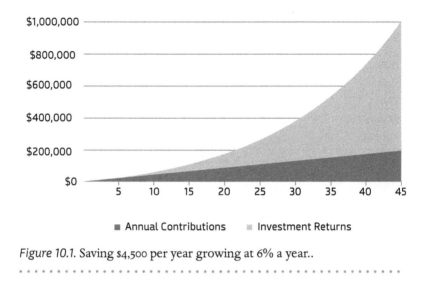

Figure 10.1. Saving $4,500 per year growing at 6% a year..

The oldest millennials will be in the workforce for another thirty years or more. To start from scratch and save $1 million over thirty years, one would need to save and invest $12,000 a year (figure 10.2).

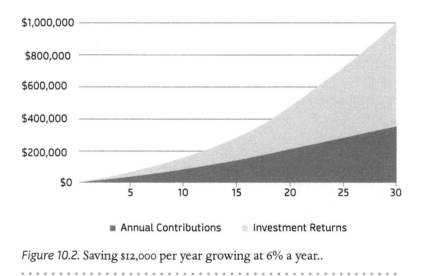

Figure 10.2. Saving $12,000 per year growing at 6% a year..

These numbers illustrate why it is so important to start early. When you start saving for retirement early, your money does more of the work for you. If you are twenty-two and you save $4,500 a year for forty-five years, you will contribute $4,500 times 45, or $202,500, by the time you are sixty-five. With investment returns (at an assumed rate of 6 percent) and compounding growth, or growth on the growth, you will have accumulated $1 million. That first $4,500 you save will grow by a factor of almost 14 over forty-five years.

If you are thirty-seven, you would need to save $12,000 a year for thirty years to reach $1 million by the same age. In this case, you would have to contribute $12,000 times 30, or $360,000. In other words, as shown in Figure 10.2, the later you start to save, the more you need to contribute to get to the same goal as someone who starts earlier. When you wait until you are thirty-seven to start, the first $12,000 you save will grow by a factor of almost 6 over thirty years

MYFL Golden Rule 9

The earlier you start to save and invest for retirement, the less you have to contribute and the more your money will work for you.

CHAPTER 11

Evaluate Your Investing Choices: What Allocation Makes Sense for You?

ONCE YOU HAVE FIGURED OUT your goals and the amount you will need to save to reach them, it is time to think about the types of investments that will help you get there. Figuring out how much money to invest in each asset class, or your asset allocation, is not a one-time exercise. Rather, it is a process that you must revisit from time to time.

For your asset allocation, begin with your time horizon. The longer you have until retirement or other milestones, the greater the allocation should be in higher-risk, higher-return assets, such as stocks. The shorter the time horizon until you need to meet an obligation, such as paying grad school tuition or making a down payment on a condo, the greater the allocation should be in more conservative investments, such as money market funds.

Think about factors that affect your profile. Consider your profession and industry with respect to your ideal allocation and make investment choices based on that information. For example, if you work in real estate, don't add to your industry exposure by investing in a lot of real estate investment trusts, or REITs. If your job is in a cyclical industry, don't invest in cyclical stocks. If your compensation is variable, take on less risk. If you have a change in your risk profile—you become a parent, your family goes from two incomes to one, you become divorced or widowed—adjust your allocations. The higher the risk in your life, the lower the risk in your investments should be.

There are two types of asset allocations. A **strategic allocation** is based on your individual needs and risk tolerance. Online asset allocation tools are available at Morningstar, Yahoo Finance, and several other financial websites. The most common allocation is 60 percent equity and 40 percent bonds. This is called a **traditional balanced allocation**. You can use a traditional balanced allocation as a starting point and then adjust your allocation given your specific needs. Another rule of thumb suggests that you take your age and subtract it from 100, which will tell you the percent of assets that you should have in stock, or equity. If you are 45 years old, this rule suggests that you have 100 minus 45, or 55 percent of your assets in stocks. Because we are all expected to live longer than our parents did, some experts suggest that you start with 110 or 120 and subtract your age.

Your asset allocation grid shows your current asset allocation and how much money you have allocated to cash and money market funds, which represents your emergency fund. Your asset allocation grid also will help you determine what changes you could make to get closer to your strategic allocation. Remember that making changes late in the year can have negative tax consequences. Making changes early in the year gives you time to offset gains with losses.

The other type of allocation is a **tactical allocation**. A tactical allocation is more opportunistic and depends on current market conditions. You can use a tactical allocation to adjust the strategic allocation. For example, you can use a tactical allocation to reduce the amount of money in asset classes that have appreciated considerably and are less attractively valued and add to asset classes that have underperformed or are more attractively valued. In this case, recall the adage that it is prudent to buy low and sell high.

CHAPTER 12

Consider Methods: Who Will Do the Investing?

O NCE YOU DETERMINE your ideal asset allocation, you need to figure out if you want to invest on your own or if you will work with a professional.

Going Solo

If you prefer to invest on your own, you can set up an account with one of the large, retail-oriented brokerage firms, such as Schwab, Fidelity, or TD Ameritrade. Invest most of your assets through the same firm to simplify the reporting process. Consolidated reports are especially helpful at tax time. In addition, you will have to consult fewer websites.

In recent years, there has been a rise in automated investment services, or "robo advisers." These firms provide online wealth management tools using technology rather than human interaction. The companies begin by surveying clients to determine risk tolerance and then use algorithms to allocate money across various exchange traded funds (ETFs.) Compared with a traditional broker or adviser relationship, these services cost less. They also offer convenience, because most companies **rebalance** accounts automatically. As investments appreciate or decline in value, the total amount in each asset class changes and deviates from your original asset allocation. Rebalancing means you add to or trim positions to bring asset class categories closer to the desired asset allocation.

As you research firms, don't forget to look at account minimums. Even if some firms may not have an account minimum, some mutual funds offered by the firm may require a minimum investment. Some automated platforms may not have a minimum account size, but charge a monthly fee. Look at the fee on an annualized basis and compare it to the amount you are investing.

Automated platforms may or may not offer advice or financial planning. If you choose to invest with an automated investment service, make sure that you understand what is in your portfolio. Remember that investing should not be a "set it and forget it" exercise. Automated platforms and online brokerage firms offer planning tools and are always introducing new types of customized financial advice. The firms usually offer different levels of help and advice. The more help and advice you want, the higher the fee. The automated platforms usually offer ETFs, but they may be theme-based or managed ETF programs, which carry a higher fee than an index-based ETF. Online brokerage firms are also expanding their managed ETF offerings.

Just as you would if you were working with a traditional broker or financial adviser, make sure that you understand all fees associated with automated platforms or online brokerage offerings. You should also ask around for referrals. Read reviews and speak with friends and family to get recommendations.

Working with a Professional

As you advance in your career and build your savings, you may choose to work with a professional. The two biggest factors guiding this decision are the amount you have to invest and the amount of help and advice you are looking for.

If you decide to work with someone, the first step is to figure out what type of financial professional you prefer. There are a couple of key distinctions between brokers and advisers:

- Brokerage firms are sometimes called broker-dealers. The firm and the individual brokers are regulated as salespeople by the Securities Exchange Act of 1934. When making decisions for clients, brokers must use a **suitability standard**. To meet a suitability standard, a broker must consider whether an investment *is suitable* for a client. In other words, the broker must consider whether an investment is appropriate, given an investor's age, financial situation, and risk tolerance.

- **Registered investment advisers**, or **RIAs**, and a firm's professionals working with clients are regulated as financial advisers, rather than as salespeople. RIAs are regulated under the Investment Advisers Act of 1940. RIAs are fiduciaries and therefore have a fiduciary duty, or are held to a **fiduciary standard**. To adhere to a fiduciary standard, an adviser must consider whether an investment *is in the best interest* of a client. A fiduciary standard is a higher standard than a suitability standard. A fiduciary standard covers the entire professional relationship and addresses issues such as potential conflicts of interest, advice on asset allocation, and fees and expenses involved. Both the RIA firm and the person associated with it must adhere to a fiduciary standard.

Anyone can use the term "adviser," and some brokers and financial planners offer investment advice relating to retirement and college planning. An investment professional who gives advice is not necessarily a fiduciary who must meet the fiduciary standard. When you meet with a prospective financial professional, ask whether he or she is a fiduciary.

Professional Credentials

Financial professionals may possess a variety of different licenses, certifications, and designations. If you are choosing to work with a financial professional, you should understand what the credentials mean.

LICENSES

The first type of credential is a license, which is required to sell securities. Licenses indicate that a financial professional has met regulatory requirements and passed an exam. The exams have long names, so people usually refer to the series number.

- To become a registered representative, professionals must pass the General Securities Representative Exam, or Series 7, and adhere to securities regulations. The Series 7 covers federal securities regulations.

- Professionals must also pass the Uniform Securities Agent State Law Examination, or Series 63, which covers securities regulations for their state.

- The Uniform Investment Adviser Law Examination, or Series 65, may be taken by professionals who give fee-based investment advice. It is not, however, a requirement for giving investment advice. Moreover, the Series 65 is not a license to sell securities. Just as not all professionals giving investment advice are RIAs, not all professionals giving investment advice have passed the Series 65 exam.

DESIGNATIONS

Designations, which include certifications, are usually an indication that a broker or an adviser has fulfilled a certain level of educational and professional experience requirements. The list of designations for financial professionals is extensive and can be confusing.

The prestige of designations and their usefulness to clients varies considerably. The Financial Industry Regulatory Authority, or FINRA, has a designation lookup feature on its website, www.finra.org/Investors/ToolsCalculators/ProfessionalDesignations/DesignationsListing. The tool is very helpful, especially because you can compare different credentials side by side. FINRA does not endorse or recommend any of these designations.

The list of designations on the FINRA website is extensive. Currently, there are 179 different designations listed. How do you determine which designations are most meaningful? As you consider a broker's or adviser's credentials, look up what is required to achieve and maintain the various designations. If you need help with retirement planning, what are the prerequisites for becoming a Certified Retirement Financial Adviser (CRFA), a Chartered Retirement Planning Counselor (CRPC), or a Personal Retirement Planning Specialist (PRPS)? The terminology can be quite confusing unless you compare the credentials side by side.

In my opinion, the most relevant designations involve an extensive study program, challenging exams, work experience requirements, a code of ethics, and continuing education. Here are some examples:

- A **Certified Public Accountant**, or CPA, is an essential credential for an accountant. Some CPAs manage money after obtaining the Personal Financial Specialist designation.
- The **Certified Financial Planner**™, or CFP®, certification indicates expertise in financial planning.

The certification is designated for fee-based professionals who provide holistic evaluations of financial profiles and develop financial plans. Some are also registered investment advisers, or RIAs, and manage clients' money for a fee.

- Professionals who complete the CFA program, which requires extensive study of various investment management topics, earn the **Chartered Financial Analyst**® credential. Many portfolio managers hold this designation.

If you decide to work with a broker or adviser, ask for referrals from family and friends. Make sure that your family and friends have worked with the broker or adviser professionally. Some friends or family may know a broker or adviser socially, but it is important that referrals come from professional experience.

You can visit regulatory websites to see if any clients have registered a complaint about a particular professional. FINRA Broker Check (www.finra.org/Investors/ToolsCalculators/Broker-Check/) is a helpful source. Check with your state regulator at the North American Securities Administrator Association, or NASAA, at www.nasaa.org/about-us/contact-us/contact-your-regulator/. The SEC adviser search (www.adviserinfo.sec.gov/IAPD/Content/Search/iapd_Search.aspx) is another good resource to consult. Check a firm's SEC Form ADV Part 2, which has a lot of information about a firm, including how much money is managed and the fee structure. The form is available on the SEC's website. The firm can also provide a copy.

Ask Questions

When you meet with a prospective broker or adviser, you need to cover certain topics. Evaluate candidates in terms of both their expertise and their interpersonal skills.

What can you tell me about your background and your practice? Ask the adviser for a basic overview of his or her practice. What is the adviser's educational and professional background? Is the adviser a broker or a fiduciary? How does the adviser get paid? What fees does he or she charge clients? What types of investments and products does the adviser use for clients' portfolios?

There is a distinction between funds and investment products from outside sources and funds and investment products from in-house, or proprietary, sources. **Proprietary products** are mutual funds or other investment funds that are managed and distributed by a broker's or adviser's firm. A broker or adviser offering only proprietary products should be a concern because incentives to use the firm's products can create a conflict of interest. Are those proprietary products in your best interest? Are investment products offered by other firms a better fit for your particular needs? Some firms offer an **open architecture** platform, which means the firm uses products from a number of vendors. In this case, make sure the vendors are truly independent and are not related, or affiliated, firms. For outside vendors, ask about compensation and revenue-sharing arrangements.

As you discuss the types of products offered, keep in mind that not all investment products are considered securities. For example, stocks, bonds, and options are securities, but fixed annuities are not—they are insurance products. The distinction is important in terms of how each is regulated and who may be able to help investors if things go wrong. The Securities and Exchange Commission cannot become involved if the investment is not a security.

Are the accounts discretionary or nondiscretionary? **Discretionary** means that the adviser can make investment decisions without consulting you first. With a **nondiscretionary** account, the broker or adviser must check with you before buying or selling anything in the account. Whether you should choose a discretionary account depends on how well you know and trust the investment professional.

How effectively does the broker or adviser explain things? Interpersonal skills are critical. In addition to having a similar investment philosophy, do you and the investment professional communicate well? The investment professional should explain investment options in plain English. To make sure that you really understand the features of an investment and how it works, try explaining the investment, its benefits, and its risks to another person.

Although it is essential that your broker or adviser have good interpersonal skills, you must keep the relationship professional. Confirm expectations and be clear that you will move your account if the manager does not do what you have requested. Everything—including any discussion of fees—should be in writing.

What is the succession plan? Who will take over if something happens to your broker or adviser or if he or she retires? Many investment professionals work in teams. You need to ensure that you are comfortable with other team members.

If the Relationship Does Not Work

When you are searching for an investment professional, the goal should be to find the right fit for the long run. If your broker or adviser does not meet your expectations, be prepared to end the relationship. If fees increase significantly, if the strategy changes without your consent, if the adviser is not responsive to your needs, or if performance consistently falls short of expectations, it makes sense to move on.

If you decide to switch to a professional at a different firm, monitor the transfer of assets very closely. The original brokerage firm will not necessarily make it easy for the new adviser or broker. In particular, make sure that cost basis information is complete. Incomplete or inaccurate information is a hassle at tax time and could result in unanticipated capital gains. Confirm that all information is complete before the new adviser starts making any changes to the portfolio. The new broker or adviser may want to sell holdings rather than have his or her performance measured based on a legacy portfolio. If your original broker or adviser manages your IRA, make sure to transfer the assets directly into another retirement account. You want to avoid an unplanned-for distribution of retirement assets. An unintended retirement account distribution could generate penalties and taxes.

CHAPTER 13

Evaluate Metrics for Potential Investments: Which Investments Are Best?

A S YOU DETERMINE WHICH investments are best for you, there are some important metrics to consider. Performance is a key factor; various ways to analyze the performance of a prospective investment or investment professional are covered in this chapter. There are also other metrics to consider that will help you determine the quality of and risks associated with different investment options.

Performance Metrics

As you evaluate investment options, start with investment performance. Whether you are looking at a fund or at the track record of a financial professional, always consider total return, or capital appreciation plus interest or dividends. You should also evaluate advisers after fees, or on a net basis. If performance is presented before fees, or on a gross basis, adjust the performance by subtracting the fee percentage.

You should also evaluate performance over different time horizons, such as for one-, three-, and five-year periods and since inception, or the beginning, of the fund. For separately managed accounts, a broker or adviser can provide investment performance information on the **composite**, or aggregation of all accounts using the same investment strategy. Performance metrics should adhere to the Global Investment Performance Standards, or GIPS, from the CFA Institute. This should be noted in the footnotes of the presentation or marketing materials.

Benchmarks

Whether you invest on your own or work with a professional, you should consider benchmarks. **Benchmarks** show how a fund or a manager performed relative to a comparable market index. Determine the most appropriate benchmark for a specific fund or a broker or adviser given the investment strategy. The Dow Jones industrial average is often quoted in the financial press, but that index consists of only thirty stocks.

The S&P 500 is the most common benchmark for equity funds or portfolios. It is actually a large-cap stock index, but it is the main benchmark for stock funds and separate accounts. Active equity managers should justify their performance—and their fee—relative to the S&P 500 because index funds based on that index are a low-cost, easily accessible alternative to active management.

Compare a fund's or a manager's performance with more specialized indexes if appropriate. If you are considering a small-cap manager or a small-cap mutual fund, you should also compare the performance of a small-cap manager or small-cap mutual fund to the Russell 2000 Index. The MSCI EAFE is a common benchmark for international stocks or funds. The Barclays US Aggregate Bond Index is the most widely used benchmark for bonds.

Peer Group Performance

In addition to evaluating funds or managers relative to a benchmark, consider how well the fund or manager performs relative to a peer group or category. Categories represent a more specialized subsection of a broader asset class. Examples include large-cap value equity, small-cap growth equity, and high-yield bonds. Morningstar is a good source for category performance.

For funds, don't simply choose the highest ranking among its peers. Being the top performer in a category is hard to sustain. Instead look for consistently good performance, a fund manager that remains in the top 50 percent of the category, and—perhaps most important—a manager that does relatively better on the downside. Good relative performance in down markets is essential.

Performance in Down Markets

Whether you choose to work with a broker or adviser or choose to manage your own investments and funds, good relative performance when times are tough is essential for the long-term growth of your investments. When evaluating investment or financial professionals, focus on the performance record during a period of market turmoil, such as in 2008, when the S&P 500 declined 37 percent. Look at how a prospective manager or fund fared during a turbulent time.

In addition to looking at challenging periods, analyze upside and downside capture for an investment, whether it is a fund or a portfolio managed by your broker or adviser. For time periods with positive market returns, **upside capture** illustrates how much a fund or portfolio gained relative to the positive performance of the benchmark or index. For periods with negative market returns, **downside capture** looks at how much the investment participated in the downside performance of the benchmark or index. If capture is less than 100 percent, the investment did not rise (upside) or fall (downside) as much as the benchmark or index. If capture is more than 100 percent, the investment rose more than (upside) or fell more than (downside) the benchmark or index. Ideally, upside capture should exceed downside capture. If it does not, you would be taking on too much risk for the expected return. For mutual funds, you can find information on upside and downside capture on Morningstar. If you work with a financial adviser, he or she should provide upside and downside capture as part of your performance reports.

Table 13.1 illustrates the importance of having less downside capture. This example assumes a loss of 37 percent in year 1, comparable to the market decline in 2008. This was the worst annual decline in the S&P 500 during my lifetime. Another noteworthy market decline occurred in the mid-1970s. In 1973 and 1974, losses totaled 37 percent over the two-year period. As illustrated in table 13.1, having less downside capture allows you to recover losses much faster.

TABLE 13.1. Impact of downside capture.

Example of full downside capture—37 percent decline

Year	Return	Ending balance	Year	Return	Ending balance
0		$1,000	0		$1,000
1	-37.0%	$630	1	-37.0%	$630
2	7.0%	$674	2	5.0%	$662
3	7.0%	$721	3	5.0%	$695
4	7.0%	$772	4	5.0%	$729
5	7.0%	$826	5	5.0%	$766
6	7.0%	$884	6	5.0%	$804
7	7.0%	$945	7	5.0%	$844
8	7.0%	**$1,012**	8	5.0%	$886
9	7.0%	$1,082	9	5.0%	$931
10	7.0%	$1,158	10	5.0%	$977
11	7.0%	$1,239	11	5.0%	**$1,026**

(continued)

TABLE 13.1. Impact of downside capture *(continued)*.

Example of less downside capture—27 percent decline

Year	Return	Ending balance	Year	Return	Ending balance
0		$1,000	0		$1,000
1	-27.0%	$730	1	-27.0%	$730
2	7.0%	$781	2	5.0%	$767
3	7.0%	$836	3	5.0%	$805
4	7.0%	$894	4	5.0%	$845
5	7.0%	$957	5	5.0%	$887
6	7.0%	**$1,024**	6	5.0%	$932
7	7.0%	$1,096	7	5.0%	$978
8	7.0%	$1,172	8	5.0%	**$1,027**
9	7.0%	$1,254	9	5.0%	$1,079

Among investors, there is a lot of discussion regarding the merits of active investing versus passive investing, such as using a market-based index fund. Active managers might find it difficult to beat a market index, especially in momentum or hot markets. But having less downside capture is a beneficial attribute of some active managers. Market-based index funds have 100 percent downside capture. As an alternative, an active manager could construct a portfolio that performs relatively better on the downside, which would mean less than 100 percent downside capture.

Other Metrics and Factors

In addition to performance, several other metrics are useful as you consider investment options. Most metrics can be used for an investable asset, a fund, or a separate account. Compare all metrics with those for the appropriate benchmark indices and with the peer group.

Valuation Metrics

For equities or equity funds, the key valuation metrics are:

- The price/earnings ratio based on prospective earnings
- Long-term earnings growth
- The price/earnings-to-growth, or PEG, ratio
- The price/book value ratio
- The dividend yield

Risk Metrics

Risk is measured by a number of factors, including beta, standard deviation, and the amount of leverage, or debt, on a company's balance sheet. Beta and standard deviation measure the volatility of returns. Leverage is usually measured by the debt/equity ratio or the debt/capitalization ratio. For the debt/capitalization ratio, capitalization refers to a company's entire capital structure and includes both equity and debt. It is not the market capitalization of the company. Substantial leverage, or debt, has an impact on a company's ability to manage through tough times. Look at the weighted average beta, standard deviation, and leverage of a portfolio or fund as an indication of the aggregate risk associated with the underlying holdings.

Monitor bond risk metrics periodically because they can change. For bonds and bond funds, consider credit rating and duration. Whether you are monitoring stocks, bonds, or a fund, remember that risk measures are not fixed but are dynamic.

Manager Tenure

Manager tenure, or the number of years that a manager has been in charge of a fund or managing separate accounts, is meaningful. There should be consistency in the person or team managing your money. Sometimes a fund is subadvised by a team of portfolio managers from another asset management firm. This is not cause for concern. A team of portfolio managers may have been chosen to subadvise a fund because they have expertise that the asset management firm lacks. Remember that you are analyzing the fund, its risk, its performance, and the experience and track record of the portfolio managers. Whether they work for the asset management firm offering the fund or are subadvising the fund is not as important.

Portfolio Attributes

For funds, the total assets under management, or AUM, and the number of holdings are important. Remember that if the assets under management are large, it may be hard for a portfolio manager to buy and sell holdings without moving the market. Mutual funds with a substantial number of holdings may not be able to perform better than the overall market. A stock fund with 350 holdings will likely perform more like the S&P 500 Index—with 500 holdings—than a fund with only 35 holdings. Each of those 35 holdings has more of an impact on performance than each of the 350 holdings in the other fund. A portfolio with 350 holdings also has a higher fee than an index fund. The same is true for bonds. For broad exposure to the bond market, investing in the Barclays US Aggregate Bond Index may be the best option.

There are other characteristics to consider:

- Look at fees compared with the average for the asset class or what other brokers or advisers are charging for a separate account.
- High portfolio turnover can lead to increased transaction costs and short-term capital gains.
- For stock funds, look at the market capitalization of the underlying holdings in the portfolio. A small-cap fund may actually contain a lot of midcap stocks.
- Identify cross holdings, or stocks or bonds that are also in other investments that you already own. You may have more concentration than you realize.

Catch a Falling Knife

There is a difference between buying a stock that is misunderstood or out of favor and buying a stock that is declining in value for a valid reason. For example, if there is evidence of fraud or accounting irregularities, the stock will likely continue to drop. Even though the valuation may be attractive, the value of the stock, like a knife, could keep falling. Whether it is a bad investment or an actual knife, catching it could be very painful.

Having a Sell Discipline or Exit Strategy

When you allocate your assets, you should focus on a long-term time horizon. At the same time, however, you also need an exit strategy—or a **sell discipline**—for every investment.

In addition to selling an investment that has become significantly overvalued, you may come across situations that could warrant exiting or selling an investment. The declining creditworthiness of a bond issuer, deteriorating company operating performance, or a significant issue with a company's management could all be reasons to sell or exit an investment. For mutual funds, it might be time to sell or redeem the funds if the manager has strayed from his or her mandate. For example, if a value manager starts buying high-growth stocks with high price/earnings multiples, he or she is not sticking with the mandate to invest in value stocks. It may be appropriate to redeem a mutual fund if its performance lags behind peers for several periods.

Never fall in love with an investment. Try to assess each investment objectively. If you don't exit when your exit strategy calls for it, your investment performance will suffer. Recognize when it is time to move on. We will cover monitoring your investments in greater detail in the next chapter.

CHAPTER 14

Monitor Your Investments: How Are You Doing?

MANAGING YOUR FINANCIAL LIFE is not a "set it and forget it" exercise. Once you have made your investing decisions and implemented your investment program, you need to monitor it on an ongoing basis.

Keep up with the financial news by reading periodicals such as the *Wall Street Journal*. There are many sources of financial news in print, online, and on television. Keeping up to date is essential as you monitor your investments.

Performance

Look at the performance of your investments regularly but not daily. Daily market fluctuations can stress you out. If you reinvest dividends and interest and do not add to or withdraw money from a separate account or fund, use the following simple formula to determine the total return percentage after fees, or on a net basis:

(Ending account balance / beginning account balance) −1

Subtracting 1 from the ratio of the ending balance over the beginning balance will give you a decimal. Then convert the decimal to a percentage. For example, 0.10 equals 10 percent. If you do not reinvest dividends or interest or add to or withdraw money from the account or fund, the performance calculation is more complex because it is based on daily balances. The manager or mutual fund can provide you the figures for net performance. Remember that financial advisers usually report performance on a gross basis, or before fees. Make sure to adjust for fees.

You should also evaluate how you are doing relative to your benchmarks. Benchmarks are helpful when monitoring individual funds or separate accounts. Benchmarks are based on indices. You can use a blended benchmark to assess the performance of a diversified pool or even your asset allocation. If your asset allocation contains 60 percent stocks and 40 percent bonds, for example, use a blended benchmark of 60 percent of the performance of the S&P 500 and 40 percent of the Barclays US Aggregate Bond Index.

As your needs change, you may require a different asset allocation. If your asset allocation changes, so should your benchmarks. If you are working with a financial professional and he or she changes a benchmark without a good reason, it is a red flag. Some brokers or advisers may try to change a benchmark if the adviser is not performing well relative to originally agreed-upon benchmarks.

Look for Overlap Across Your Investments

From time to time, check to see if there is overlap or redundancy across your investments. As portfolio managers make changes to their funds, some holdings could pop up in more than one of your investments. Morningstar and other online resources can provide information on the overlap in different mutual funds.

Rebalance

Revisit and update your asset allocation grid periodically. You may have to rebalance, or reallocate, your portfolio on occasion. The returns for your various investments will vary. Some investments will increase in value more than others. As a result, the amount of assets in some asset classes will grow more than others. Over time, your current asset allocation will move away from your original strategic allocation.

Look at your needs and how your investments have performed and revisit your sell discipline. You may buy more shares of stock or of a fund or add to a position. You may decide to sell some of your holdings or trim a position.

Portfolio managers maintain a **watch list** of investments that they have analyzed and would like to buy but that may be too expensive. You can do this too. Look for opportunities to invest in stocks, bonds, or funds that you have monitored and that have become more attractively valued. When you rebalance, you can trim positions or asset classes that have appreciated and add to positions or asset classes that have not appreciated and are more attractively valued.

It is important not to rebalance with every minor diversion from your asset allocation targets. Rebalancing can result in transaction costs. You should not rebalance at the end of the year, because you might generate a taxable gain. Earlier in the year, there is time to offset a gain with a capital loss.

Going Forward

Not only is it important to monitor your investments, you also need to take a step back from time to time and reevaluate your financial profile and your individual needs. As you probably have realized by now, managing your financial life is not a linear process. It is an ongoing, circular process. You don't finish the task and set it aside. Rather, you need to regularly revisit the steps outlined in this book.

Maintain your system and reevaluate your financial profile and needs. Stay up to date with your investments and what is going on in the financial world. Managing your financial life is a dynamic process, not a static one.

Managing your financial life requires an investment of your time as well as your money. If you make this process part of your routine, you can relax, knowing that you are indeed in control of your financial life.

Notes

1. Bureau of Labor Statistics, "National Longitudinal Survey of Youth 1997," updated 2016.

2. Forrester Research, Inc. Data Mobile Payments Forecast, 2016 to 2021 (US) 2017.

3. Federal Reserve Board of Governors, 2016 Survey of Consumer Finances (New York: Federal Reserve, 2016).

4. Federal Reserve Bank of New York, *Quarterly Report on Household Debt and Credit 2017*: Q4 (New York, Federal Reserve, 2017).

5. "Trends in the Expenses and Fees of Funds, 2016," ICI Research Perspective vol. 23, no. 3 (May 2017).

6. Social Security Administration Periodic Life Expectancy, https://www.ssa.gov/OACT/TR/2009/lr5a3.html#h

7. "Social Security Administration Retirement Benefits, https://www.ssa.gov/benefits/retirement/

Index

purchases, record of, 6–7, 9
puts, **85**

quality, as a factor in evaluating securities, 98

rate of return on retirement investments, 133–35
real estate investment trusts. *See* REITs
real estate, as an illiquid asset, 60
realize a loss on an investment, **67**
rebalancing accounts, **146**
recourse loan, **37**
redemption, **93**
registered investment advisers (RIAs), **147**
reinvested dividends/interest, 107, 163–64
REITs, 67, **88,** 142
relative return, 89
retained earnings, **81,** 82
retirement accounts, 5–6, 16
    withdrawing ages, 110
    consolidating, 109
retirement savings, 133, 139
    borrowing from, 129
    calculating needs, 122
    guidelines, 122–23
    planning for, 119–24
    sources of, 120
returns for equity and bond benchmarks, 136–37
    at 6 percent annual rate, *138*
risk, **58,** 59. *See also specific types of risk,*
    e.g., counterparty risk
    assessing, 49
risk management, **52**
risk profiles, 142
risk tolerance, **52**
risk, geopolitical, 84
robo advisers. *See* automated investment services
Roth 401(k)s, **109**

Roth IRAs, **109,** 110
    conversions, 110
    inheritance of, 111
    taxes on, 66
Rule of 72, **134,** 135
Rule of 7s, **134,** 135
Russell 2000 Index
    as benchmark for small-cap performance, 156

S&P 500, 135, 164
    as alternative to active management, 156
salary multiples, use of for retirement planning, 122–23
sales load, **63**
savings plans. *See also specific types of plans, e.g.,* retirement savings
    goal-setting for, **128**
    impact of, **126**
secondary market, **70,** 71
securities
    defined, 29
Securities and Exchange Commission, 151
    adviser search (website), 150
    Form ADV, Part 2, 150
Securities Exchange Act of 1934, 147
securities *vs.* investment products, 151
sell discipline, 165
"sell in May and go away," 59
sell short, **89,** 92

SEP IRAs. *See* simplified employee pension plans
separate accounts, **92,** *95*
    S&P 500 as benchmark for, 156
separately managed accounts, 156
short. *See* sell short
simplified employee pension (SEP) plan, **109**
small-cap companies, 94

About the Author

Nancy Doyle is the founder of The Doyle Group, LLC; she has thirty years' experience in wealth management, investments, finance, and consulting. She is a graduate of Georgetown University, received her MBA from University of Michigan's Ross School of Business, and holds the Chartered Financial Analyst® (CFA®) designation. In addition to her passion for financial literacy, she is active in her community. Ms. Doyle, her husband, and their two children live near Chicago.

CPSIA information can be obtained
at www.ICGtesting.com
Printed in the USA
FFHW02n1326070918
48282890-52082FF